Leo

Leo Adam Kraemer

Copyright © 2018 Kenneth L. Kraemer
All rights reserved.
ISBN-13: 978-1982048501

DEDICATION

To the mother I never knew
Grace Ring Kraemer

CONTENTS

	Preface	i
	Acknowledgements	iii
1	Parents and Family	1
2	Childhood	13
3	Marriage	27
4	Work Life at EKS	37
5	Children	51
6	Weddings	61
7	Retirement	75
8	Letters	93
9	Memories	99
10	Family in the Census	111
11	Ancestors and Descendants	113
	References	119
	Index	121

PREFACE

This book is by, and about, Leo Kraemer. It is based on interviews with Leo between 1986-1988. It is written in the first person as though Leo was writing because the text is mostly as he said it. As editor, I have mainly organized it, added commentary, inserted footnotes and selected photos to complement his text.

Our discussions followed a time line from his earliest memories to the time of the interviews. At best, this is a poor snapshot of the person, but I thought it was important to do for nieces, nephews and others who knew him only a little, or not at all, but would have liked to.

In working on the Kraemer family genealogy (*Wisconsin Kraemers, I, II and III*), I have often wished that I had pages from a diary or letters that Leo wrote so I could get more insight into his thoughts, emotions and character. I was 18 when I left Plain and returned only every few years for a week or so. I really did not know him well and, hence, was motivated to try to create something for myself and others.

Leo was a quiet and independent man who did not often show his emotions. He loved Lucy very much. He called her "little doll" because she was small and light. Everyone in the family remembers how he would embrace her, kiss her and swing her around on Sunday mornings after church. He never knew his mother as she died when he was only two years old. He developed a deep attachment to his aunt Frances Weidner because he lived with her for several years after his mother died. He very much felt that aunt Frances was like a mother to him. When his father married again, he never developed an attachment to this new mother who was a spinster until she married Peter Kraemer at age 35. She appeared a disciplinarian, possibly because she didn't know how to cope with all the children she inherited, and she appeared gruff possibly because she only spoke German.

Leo was the youngest in a family of 10 children, but separated from the children of Peter's first wife - all boys - by six years and three older sisters. He never quite felt part of the first family, but was close to his sisters. He was highly respected by all the men he worked with when a foreman on road construction.

His dream was to have his own farm. Immediately after marriage, he rented several farms but was not able to make enough money to accumulate savings that would enable him to buy a farm. So, he went to work on road construction for his brother's firm, Edward Kraemer and Sons. The dream of being an independent farmer remained with him his whole life as he often wondered, as we all do, how different his life might have been had he been able to take that different path. Mother and dad would drive by their first farm in later years and express the wish that they had been able to succeed in farming. But these were the depression years and many people didn't make it – many lost their farms all together.

After a week of struggling for breath and back aches as his body was shutting down, he died quietly and alone in The Meadows assisted living home in Spring Green, WI. Although family members had been present the entire week, and spent a lively day with him on his last day, he chose to die during a brief period when he was alone. We think maybe the loner in him wanted it that way, but it added to our sense of loss.

Ken Kraemer, Newport Coast, California, 2018

ACKNOWLEDGEMENT

It is important to acknowledge the contribution of the other family members to this book: Virginia, Doris, Phyllis, Jan and Ron Kraemer and some of their children. These contributions include photos, letters, and memories. None of the letters and memories were written directly for this book. Rather, they were written over the years in normal correspondence with Leo and Lucy or for special occasions such as the 50th, 60th or 70th wedding anniversaries, and are collected here.

1. PARENTS AND FAMILY

PARENTS

I was born on March 21, 1905 at my dad's farm in Wilson Creek, Town of Spring Green, Sauk County, Wisconsin. At that time, most children were born in the home rather than in the hospital.

My mother was Grace Ring. I did not know her because she died when I was two years old. My brother Edward Kraemer once told me that "she was the sweetest and kindest woman he ever knew." Grace was the daughter of Adam Ring and Frances (Franzisca) Roetzer who lived close to the Paul Kraemer farm- just over the Franklin Township line in Troy Township.

All the Rings [except Michael] had all been born in Bavaria.[1] They and immigrated to America in 1883. The family consisted of five girls and two boys. Frances, Anna, Grace, Theresa, Elizabeth, Katharine, John and Mike. Elizabeth and Katharine became nuns. Anna was the first wife of my dad. Grace was dad's second wife. Frances Ring married George P. Schutz. Theresa married a McMahan from North Dakota. John Ring lived in Mazomanie; I don't remember who he married. Mike ran the general store in Plain and married Christina Haas.

---

[1] A daughter named Frances died in Germany in 1878.

The Adam Ring Family, after March 1898

Top row, L-R: Theresa (John McMahan), Frances (George P. Schutz), John, Michael (Christina Gruber), Grace (Peter Kraemer). Bottom row, L-R: Elizabeth (Sister Winibald OSF), Adam (the father), Frances (Roetzer, the mother), Katharina (Sister Susana OSF) Ring. Photo from Damian Kraemer. NOTE: We believe that Anna Ring is not in this photo and that it was taken after her death in March 1898. The person previously identified as Anna Ring is Theresa Ring.

My father was Peter Kraemer, the eldest son of Paul Kraemer. He was two years old when he came to America and grew up on their farm on Butternut Road just off Highway B east of Plain.

Paul Kraemer family photo, circa 1893

On chair: Mary Kraemer Laubmeier, Paul and Walburga Kraemer, Theresa Kraemer Meister. **Standing**: George Laubmeier, Peter, Joseph, John, Margaret Kraemer and Martin Meister.

Anna Ring was dad's first wife. There were married in 1899 and lived on the home farm in Wilson Creek. Anna had six children and died from confinement about age 32, a week after giving birth to her last child--Ben Kraemer. [Anna was born March 25, 1866 and died March 21, 1898.[2]]

Peter Kraemer and Anna Ring, 1888

---

[2]She was born in Germany the same year that Paul Kraemer and his family came to the U.S.

Grace Ring was dad's second wife. He married her in 1890, about a year after Anna died. Grace was seven years younger than Anna, so that made her about 25 when she married dad. They also lived on the home farm and she died at the age of 34.

Peter Kraemer and Grace Ring, 1899

Photo from Doris Bindl.

She died from TB, but she had been ill for some time before that. She had had two amputations of her leg from gangrene which set in from a poorly handled injury to her heel. The amputations were performed at La Crosse which was the only hospital in the area at the time. She was about six months pregnant at the time she died, and the baby did not survive.

> Leo's recollection is incorrect on several points above. First, we do not know exactly what was wrong with Grace's foot/leg. We do know that she had some sort of operation in Madison in February 1904 because it is mentioned in a *Home News* article below. In addition, Dr. Bossard of Spring Green was continually re-bandaging her foot and then her leg for over a year afterwards. Possibly she had her foot and then her leg amputated. We contacted the records department of both the La Crosse and Madison hospitals that existed in 1904 to discover the nature of any operation. These hospitals had no records going back that far.
>
> | Mrs. Peter Cramer, who has been suffering with an abcess on one of her limbs, was obliged to go to Madison, where she underwent an operation. Mr. Cramer has returned from the city and reports that his wife is improving. | Source: *Weekly Home News*, 25 February 1904. The article refers to Mrs. Peter Kraemer. There was no Mrs. Peter Cramer in Plain at the time and the story is reported under the section on news about Plain. |
> |---|---|
>
> Second, grace was pregnant at the time of the operation(s), but the baby was born and survived – that baby was Leo. Third, there is no evidence suggesting that Grace was pregnant at the time she died. For example, her death record only says that she died of TB and had been treated for TB for two years.

Grace was born on 29 January 1873 and died January 27, 1907.

Katherine Eckstein was Peter's third wife. They were married in 1909 and lived on the home farm until dad sold it to Ben and moved to town in the 1940s. Then they lived next to dad's brother - Joe Kraemer - in Plain until dad become too old to take care of himself. Then he moved in with my sister Anna and Clem Frank, who lived on the street that goes by the church [Nachreiner Street].

Peter Kraemer and Katherine Eckstein, 1909

Source: Doris Bindl.

My brothers and sisters

Anna and Pete had seven children:
        John Leo (Isabella Hutter and Matilda Haas)
        Edward (Gisela Frank)
        Albert "Doc" (Matilda Nachreiner)
        Anthony (died as child)
        Frank (Mary Bayer)
        Alphonse (Mary Frank)
        Ben (Elsie Peters)
Grace and Pete had four children:
        Anna "Annie" (Clem Frank)
        Elizabeth "Lizzie" (Albert Liegel and Lynn Schult)
        Esther (Ted Frank)
        Leo (Lucy Bauer)

Kate and Pete had two children, but they died young. The oldest fell backwards into a kettle[3] of water and lard when about two years old. The younger one died in about three months from child's illness [gastroenteritis or inflammation of the stomach and intestines]. The children's deaths occurred on the home farm in Wilson Creek.

My Dad

My dad had two farms. When he went to town he sold one to Frank and another to Ben for about ten thousand dollars each [actually $8000]. Ben had lots of debt on his farm. The bank had the loan on the land; Pete had the loan on the buildings and Pete Peters (Elsie Kraemer's dad) had the loan on the farm equipment. Ben was not able to make a go of the farm and had to sell it for $6,000. He was not able to pay back the loans on the farm. [See

---

[3] Use of the word "kettle" here is misleading. It does not refer to a kettle with a spout such as one would use on a stove to heat water, but probably to an open rectangular boiler used for heating a large quantity of water. The death certificate only says accidental burning.

Wisconsin Kraemers III, Chapter 7, Benjamin Kraemer and Elsie Peters for a more complete discussion].

Peter Kraemer family, circa 1917*

Top, L>R: Benedict, Frank, Edward, Albert, Alphonse, John. Middle, L>R: Elizabeth (Liegel), Anna (Frank), Esther (Frank). Bottom, L>R: Peter, Leo, Katherine (Eckstein) *The 1917-year estimate for the photo is based on the fact that Peter's wife in the photo is Kate Eckstein (married in 1909) and Leo Kraemer (born in 1905) looks to be about 12 years old.

Timeline of major events in Leo's life

1898	Peter Kraemer marries Grace Ring
1905	Leo is born to Peter and Grace on the Wilson Creek farm
1907	Leo's mother dies and he lives with aunt Frances Weidner
1910	Leo returns home and lives with Peter and Kate Eckstein
1920	Leo is living at home, student, age 14 (1920 U.S. Census)
	Leo starts working outside the farm
1923	Leo goes to work for Ted Frank
1925	Lucy goes to work for Ted Frank
1926	Leo marries Lucy Bauer, age 21 (marriage certificate)
	Leo and Lucy rent the Clem Frank farm in Wilson Creek
1927	Leo and Lucy rent the Prouty farm north of Plain
1928	Virginia born, February 20
1929	Leo starts work for Edward Kraemer, age 24
	Stock market crash and beginning of the Great Depression
1930	Leo and Lucy rent the "little house". in Plain (1930 Census)
1931	Doris is born, 29 March
1933	Leo and Lucy buy the Martin house in Plain
1934	Phyllis is born, 1 February
1935	Leo and Lucy get loan from Ed for their house
1936	Kenneth is born, October 29
1938	Jan is born, 11 July
1941	Leo and Lucy pay off loan on their house
1944	Leo spends a year crushing rock for an airport in Covington, KY
1946	Ron is born, 17 April
1975	Leo retires from EKS (Edward Kraemer and Sons) at age 70
1976	50th wedding anniversary
1986	60th wedding anniversary
1993	Leo and Lucy move to Westbrook in Plain
1996	70th wedding anniversary
1997	Lucy moves to Greenway Manor nursing home in Spring Green
1998	Leo moves to The Meadows assisted living in Spring Green
2000	Lucy dies at Greenway Manor
2002	Leo dies at The Meadows

LEO FROM AGE 3 TO AGE 90+

From L>R and then down: Age 3-4; Age 10, First Communion photo; Age 15, Confirmation photo, Age 21, Wedding photo; Age 39-40, holding Ken; Age 55; Age 70; Age 80, Age 90+

LOCATION OF FAMILY FARMS

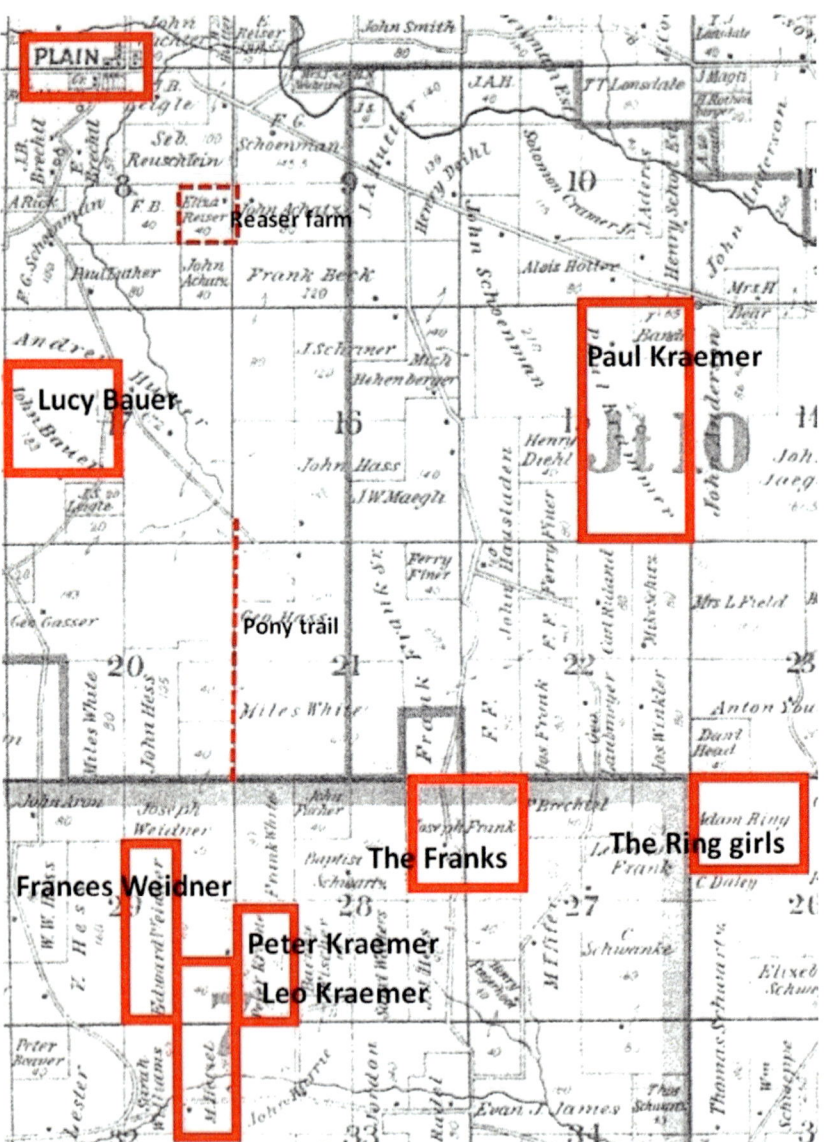

1893 plat map showing portions of Franklin, Troy and Spring Green Townships.

2. CHILDHOOD

MY BIRTH MOTHER

My mother was Grace Ring. She was the sister of dad's first wife. I was born on my dad's farm in Wilson Creek. I was about two years old when my mother died. I never knew her.

Grace, 1898   **Grace, age 26, 1899**

MY AUNT, "MY REAL" MOHER

After my mother died, my dad could not take care of us little kids so Lizzie, Ester and I went to live with my aunt Frances Weidner who lived on the farm next door to dad. Frances Weidner was the "Franzisca" Kraemer who came to the U.S. along with my dad in 1866. She was eight years old at the time she came, so she remembered the whole trip. She was born in 1858 in Irlach, Barvaria in the original Kraemer home at house number 27 and she died in 1928 at the age of seventy on her farm in Wilson Creek. Her husband Edward had died already in 1892 from pneumonia.

    She was forty years old when we moved in with her and she already had two children of her own—Mary and Jack Weidner. Mary married Ferry Hausladen; Lloyd Hausladen was her only child. "Abbie" Weidner was Jack's son. The girl was four or five and the boy two years old when their dad died. Frances then ran the farm by herself. She milked the cows, cleaned the barn, hauled the milk to the Wilson Creek cheese factory, and so on. My dad and the neighbors did the heavy work for her. She canned fruit and vegetables and her house was always clean.

Frances at 17 years

Frances at 45 years

Leo Kraemer, circa 1908-09 (3 or 4 years old)

Source: Doris Bindl. Note the iron-wheeled wagon and Leo's long hair. The photo was not taken at the Pete Kraemer home; perhaps the Weidners or another home.

    I couldn't have had a nicer place to stay. I really liked my aunt and she was really the only real mother that I had. I usually got everything I wanted. I remember once that I was standing on a chair and began singing and all at once Frances and her daughter saw me and rushed to get me because they thought I might fall off the chair.

Frances had an apple orchard and in the fall, she would cut up the apples and slice them and put them on a white cloth and put them on top of the wood pile to dry out. She put a cheese cloth over them, so the birds couldn't get at them. She would carry them out to the wood pile in the morning and take them in at night, so they wouldn't get dew on them. I would crawl up on the wood pile and snitch the drying apples. She usually had about a 35-pound sack of the apples every year and would use the apples for making pie in the winter.

One time I had to take a pail of water back to my aunt's son Jack who was plowing in the field. I stopped on the way to see the colt. The colt came up to me and wanted a drink of water and he drank most of it. I couldn't get his head out of the pail and so there was very little water left. I didn't want to go back and get some more so I took what I had left to Jack. When I got the water to Jack, he drank it and said why didn't you bring more. I said I did, but the colt drank the rest. He spit tobacco thru his teeth and said "giddy-up" and went right on plowing.

I used to be pigeon-toed when I was young. I would run and catch my toe in my pants leg and fall. I don't know how I got over it, but somehow, I did.

A RUDE AWAKENING

I stayed with Frances until I was five years old. Then I went home to dad's farm and his new wife. I don't know how I got there from my aunt's. The next day I was in bed sleeping. It was in the fall and, so it was dark outside. She yelled upstairs to me, "Leo get up." It was dark, and I didn't want to get up, so I turned over and went back to sleep. Next thing I knew, the covers were pulled back and I got the pancake turner on my bare rear. That was my introduction to my new mother. I never cared for her. She was a strict woman and we kids were kind of wild. I stayed away from

Kate as much as I could. Whenever I could, I ran over to my aunt's house, which was the farm next door in Wilson Creek.

CHILDHOOD MEMORIES

Sleigh riding. Ed make me a sled with wooden runners and a piece of steel on the bottom.

Cracking hickory nuts. I had picked a 12-pint pail and had to crack them all.

Listening to my echo. I would yell and listen to my echo from hill to hill.

We didn't have electric lights. We had a battery-operated light plant in the basement.

We had a hand pump for the house and a windmill to pump the water for the barn.

I remember my dad making staves for barrels and cutting railroad ties. It was a way to make money beyond farming.

There were lots of woods next to the house and barn. They had to be cut down to clear the land for crops or grazing. I remember the stumps were there a long time because clearing the land was a difficult and long process.

Smoking a corn cob pipe when 10 years old. Pete had a pail of tobacco sitting on the cellar steps. He always smoked a pipe in the winter, first thing in the morning. I didn't have to do chores because I was the youngest, so when no one was around, I smoked one of his pipes. One day, Kate saw the stem of the pipe sticking out of my coat pocket and took it away, but I got another one.

I can't kick about my childhood. We had it about as good as most people. Most people didn't have their wives die so much. Pete had the worst luck of anybody in Wilson Creek. Really, I couldn't say I was unhappy. Dad always treated me good. I just didn't like the stepmother. Esther and Annie also moved in with Kate. They couldn't do anything right for her and were always in trouble with her. She wasn't our real mother and so that had a lot to do with how we felt about her. She didn't feel good in the last years; she had gall stones and was too heavy to be operated on, so she just died with it

She didn't have an easy life either. She got married and he [Pete] had that big family and she had to cook and wash for everybody. You had to turn the washing machine by hand and turn the wringer by hand. It was hard work. You also had to iron everything after washing. Everybody lived at home most of the time except John. Ed and Albert went out working during the week but came home every weekend. Later we all went out working.

Dad died playing cards – the game of 66. He was playing cards with George P. Schutz. They lived nearby in Wilson Creek and were brothers-in-law. Both were married to Ring sisters. Two married Pete and the other married George. Pete had a heart attack and fell of the chair and died right there.

Church

We went to St. Luke's church in Plain by horse and buggy. When I was young, we went to the church down by the old picnic grounds [The location of the first three churches: 1861, 1884 and 1906].

St. Luke's church complex, circa 1908

After the 1908 cyclone, the parsonage and church were gone. The grounds were used for church picnics.

We got a car around 1914 or 1915 and then used that to go to church. There was nothing but dirt roads out in the country. There was a gravel road from Mike Bindl's to town and a section of County B on the road to Richland Center at the hill after the Lins farm.

Two Schools

I went to the Catholic school in Plain during the summer and to the one-room public school in Wilson Creek during the winter. I walked to school. I didn't walk, I ran most of the time.

Sister Walburta was teacher for grades 1, 2, 3 and 4. Sister Leocadia was the teacher for grades 5, 6, 7, and 8. Lucy had her too. [Phyllis, Ken and Norine had Sister Leocadia too but only for seventh grade]. Florence Needham and Mrs. George Bauer were the two public school teachers that I knew in Wilson Creek.

The Catholic school was down by the church at the old picnic grounds. The church and school were blown down in 1918. There was no high school in the old school, but they started high school when the new school was built in town after the tornado [the present-day St. Luke school on Nachreiner St.]

I couldn't go to the public school in Plain because it required one to speak English and we only spoke German at home. The Catholic school conducted classes all in German, but it was high German and I didn't understand it. You didn't get a report card. You just got a crack across the hands or the back, or the head. The nuns really were mean. We had German reading, bible history, geography and oral arithmetic. I never could get it [the arithmetic]. We had English too.

We went to the Catholic school until about Thanksgiving and then started again around Easter. I went as far as the eighth grade. At that time that was as far as we could go in school.

We never had any plays or programs like they do now. It was strictly book-learning. Now they have so much more to look forward to than we did.

In grade school, I was seated with Hammer Walsh. One day he let out a yell and the teacher said, "Who did that?" Hammer pointed to me and I got sent to the principal's office. She said, "Why are you here?" I explained what happened and then Hammer really got a talking to.

We always had to milk cows before we went to school. We had to take turns pumping water for the cattle, 200 strokes each [person]. That was an everyday job and everyone in the family got a turn.

I walked four and a half miles to the Catholic school in Plain. I didn't walk; I usually ran. I would cut through the woods on the "pony" trail.[4] I remember running thru a blackberry patch one time and stepping on a snake head another time. The snake coiled around my leg, but I kept running and it let go.

When I was older, one time I went out to hitch up the horses to go to church. I wasn't supposed to go near the horses and I was barefoot besides. Old Charlie stepped back and put his shoed foot right on the front of my foot. It swelled up something awful and I had to put on shoes to go to church. I was praised for hitching up the horses, but I didn't dare say anything about my swollen foot.

When I was going to school, they had a school bus which operated down in Barney Bindl's area [Mill Road east of Plain]. It was a long wagon with a cab on it. It was pulled by a team of three horses and each farmer had to take turns driving for a week. It went from the George Volk farm (the Herbert Bindl, Vernon Bindl, Kenny Bindl farm) up to St. Luke's every day. The Volk/Bindl farm was the dividing line between Town of Franklin and Town of Troy.

Church picnics and other socials

Every year there was a church picnic. They were primarily social affairs although they also were aimed at raising money for the school or church. A few people would give prizes such as a hog or

---

[4] The pony trail ran through the woods up and down a large sweeping hill and connected with a road into Plain. It was still a dirt road with deep ruts and rarely graded when I was young. Now it is paved.

a calf to be given away in a raffle. The picnics were usually held around July 4th and lasted several days. They were held down by Lena Reasers (Dead End Road off County B east of Plain by the current vet's office) because there was a nice big clearing and nice trees around it. They set up the tables in the trees. They hauled in wood cook stoves. They had games and drawings. We would have chicken, potatoes, pies and so forth.

Reaser Farm

Source: Thering, 1982, p. 17.

The picnics also were held on the hill where St. Luke's church is located now. There used to be trees on that hill.

After the old church blew down in 1917, we had the picnics at the old church and school grounds. The meals were held in the old school building which was left standing after the tornado. There was a band that would play at these events. Phillip Bettinger, Joe Bauer, Dutch Ruhland and Alphons Kraemer were in the band. There is a picture of the band in Hilda Thering's book about Plain.

Joe Frank's new barn in Wilson Creek was built in 1915. It had a nice smooth floor and they had a barn dance there after it was finished. Somebody reported to Father Pesch that we had the barn dance on a Sunday and he raised hell in a sermon the next Sunday and said we all had to go to confession. We got 10-15 rosaries penance for going to the dance. We weren't supposed to go dancing from when we sowed the oats until everything was off the field. Easter Monday was usually the last dance. There was just too much work to do. There were no movies or radio; only some organs, record players, pianos, and accordions, but you weren't even supposed to play these instruments on Sunday.

Leo's first communion photo, circa 1913

Source: Doris Bindl, 2015. Leo appears to be around 8-10 years old.

Teenage, dancing, girls

I didn't have friends when I was a teenager. People mostly went to taverns to drink and I didn't like to go to taverns or drink. My friends were my cousins. I used to go to movies in Spring Green once a week. I went with Lucy and Marie (Weitzer) Heiss and George Schutz. I went with others too.

When I was 13, I went to the Spring Green fairgrounds with dad. It was 1918. I remember the date because dad got a new model-T Ford that year. The present-day Spring Green golf course used to be a stockyard and fair grounds. There was a big grandstand. There were horse races, bands, judging of animals, beer stands, and food stands as well as crafts. During the day I got tired and went to go to the car to lay down. When I got to the parking lot there were so many model-T's that I couldn't find dads, so I had to go back to the fairgrounds. Dr. Watson, the vet, used to race horses, but I don't remember who the rest were. I think they were from out of town.

When I was 18, I went to Devil's Lake with Herb Kraemer[5], the Ederer boys and a few more guys. They all got into the water and started swimming toward a raft. I didn't know how to swim but headed after them, and suddenly there was a drop-off and I couldn't touch bottom. I started swimming or dog paddling and somehow made it to the raft. After the guys had enough on the raft, they jumped in and headed back to shore. That left me alone and I had to get back too. I made it, but I never went into water over my waist again.

I liked to dance but I was afraid to go out on the dance floor because I was always concerned that I was not as good as the others. A girl in Loretto had her eye on me, and I danced with her at dances, but that was all there was to it. A girl from Lancaster wanted me to take her to a prom. I took Clara Bayer (Mrs. Dick Ederer) to a movie two times. Her sister, Mary Bayer, was married to my brother Frank, which is how I knew her. Frank lived on the farm next to Ben in Wilson Creek.

---

[5]Herb Kraemer was a cousin – one of John Kraemer's sons – who lived in Wyoming Valley across the Wisconsin River from Spring Green.

One time I was heading towards old George Schutz's farm (later the Fink Feiner farm in horseshoe bend) when young Georg Schutz[6] and some friends came along the road. I turned out, so they could pass, and they stopped, and we talked. They said they were going for a drive and I should come along. George took the keys from my car and, so I had to go along or be left behind. So, I left my car and got in with them. There were six of us there. We drove around and went over to Spring Green and back. That was a long way in that time.

When we got back Helen Diehl fought George for the key to my car and then asked me to take her home. She lived near me and, so I took her home. That is all there was to it. Lucy always felt there was more to it, probably because Helen was forward (see Helen Diehl in confirmation photo below). My first real date and my first kiss was with Lucy (Bauer). I never really went with anybody else except Lucy.

Helen Diehl   **Leo Kraemer (15)**   **Lucy Bauer (16)**
              (unknown girl)

These photos are cut from "Confirmation Class, Plain, Wisconsin, October 12, 1920, Spring Green Studio, C.H. Stumpf, Prop."

---

[6] George Schutz's mother [Frances Ring] and my mother [Grace Ring] were sisters so we were first cousins. They were both the sisters of Mike Ring.

Work away from home

When John Kraemer's first wife (Isabelle Hutter) died in 1921, Kate (Pete's third wife) went to take care of John's kids. When Kate went to John's, I was 16 and went to work for a year for Clem and Annie Frank who lived on a farm near dad's farm at the time. After a year Clem left the farm and opened a butcher shop in town (Buddy Weitzer later opened a grocery store there).

When Clem moved to town I went to work for Ted Frank. That was 1923 and I was about 18 when I went to work for Ted. I worked there about 3 years. During this time, Frank Kraemer had a rupture operation and, so I went to work for him from about March through Spring. Frank Kraemer lived on the present Rudy Feiner farm at this time. I was there about 3-4 months and we made moonshine.

Then Ted wanted to make moonshine because he couldn't make money at farming anymore. I would drive over from Frank's place to Ted's place at night and make moonshine. We had 10-12 fifty-gallon barrels in the ice house. One week I didn't do anything but make moonshine. Frank got half, and Ted got half. Plain was all moonshine country. Ray Ring hauled moonshine to Chicago. Other guys came from Madison, Milwaukee, and Chicago and picked up the moonshine from farmers. That was about 1921-1924.

Sometime in that three-year period with Ted, I worked for Ed Kraemer in the carpenter business for about three months. I didn't like carpenter work because it was hard and involved heavy lifting and I was too small.

One winter I went to help Ben Kraemer on his farm in Wilson Creek. We cut cordwood that winter and when we were done, I went back to work for Ted again and stayed there until Lucy and I got married.

All the fieldwork was done with horses. You would cut the grain with a binder and put it up in shocks. When it was dried out after four weeks you would put it in a stack. Usually there would be about two grain stacks about 30 feet high, and about 15 feet in diameter. The threshing machine would be put between these stacks and the shocks and would separate the grain from the straw and throw the straw into a stack which ended up being about 75 feet long, 25 feet wide, and about 15 feet high. Seven to eight neighbors always helped with threshing. Neighbors also helped with cutting wood. That usually was a full day of work at each farm. I bought my first Model T in 1924.

Leo, Lucy and Model T, circa 1924-25

Unidentified, George Schutz, Marie Weitzer, Leo Kraemer, Tootsie Hutter, Devils Lake

3. MARRIAGE

I never really went with anybody else except Lucy. I met Lucy in 1925. We got married in 1926. We were both 21 when we got married.

Roads were dirt. It was the 13th of April and we had to turn out for the mud holes. One time I took her home and went the long way around. The road was smooth, but it covered a mud hole and there I sat in the mud up to the running board. I went into Robinsons [local farmer] and told him I was stuck. He was washing his feet. He pulled me out with a horse. I thought it would cost about five dollars, but he didn't charge me a thing.

The night before we got married we got stuck and I had to push out the car. I yelled at mother, "Don't put the gas on so much!" She got mad and said, "If I knew you were going to yell at me like that I never would have agreed to marry you."

LUCY'S VIEW OF LEO

[Leo didn't talk much about their courtship or marriage, so we use Lucy's account recognizing that it does not correspond completely with what Leo said in Chapter 2.

I knew Leo all through school. He always went by our house when he went to school. He would go through the woods because that made it closer. When I was twenty, I went to Ted and Ester Frank's in October 1925 to help Ester after she had her daughter

Alice. I stayed at Franks until February and then I went back to the home farm. It was at the Franks that I met dad. I had known him before that however.

I really was going with a guy when I went to work at Ted Franks. One night when we got through milking I walked up to the stone building where Leo always took some milk to the skunk and looked at it. On the way back, he asked me if I wanted to ride along to Spring Green to a band concert, so I did. I had called to Spring Green to ask a girl friend of mine to meet me, and we got together to walk around, and when it got to be 10:00 o'clock I went to the car and it wasn't long when Leo came too, so that is how it started. I ditched the guy and started with Leo.

We went to Milwaukee one fall. Leo visited Al Porter and I visited Leona Butler, a girl I met working at Spring Green. Later we went to dances. She also came to visit me, many times, and attended our sixtieth wedding anniversary. I was very surprised because she had a sick husband and came from Milwaukee where they were living then. Our 60th anniversary was celebrated July 6, 1986.

We were married April 13, 1926. There were 14 people at the wedding dinner:

>Father Camera
>Father Surges
>Pete Kraemer and Kate
>My mother, Margaret Bauer
>Johnny Bauer [my brother]
>Christina Weitzer [my sister]
>Ella Bauer [my sister]
>Ted and Esther [Leo's sister and husband]
>George Schutz, the best man; George was a cousin and a neighbor; we lived in the same neighborhood when growing up.

Marie Weitzer Heiss, the maid of honor, was my niece; she lived with us when we were little and was like a sister to me although she was the daughter of my sister Christina.

Leo and Lucy wedding

>R: Leo Kraemer, Lucy Bauer, George Schutz, Marie Weitzer. Source: Marriage certificate Register No. 467, April 7, 1926, Register of Deeds, Sauk County, Baraboo, WI. Photo from Doris Bindl.

Leo and Lucy marriage certificate
Transcription: License No. 5364   Register No. 467

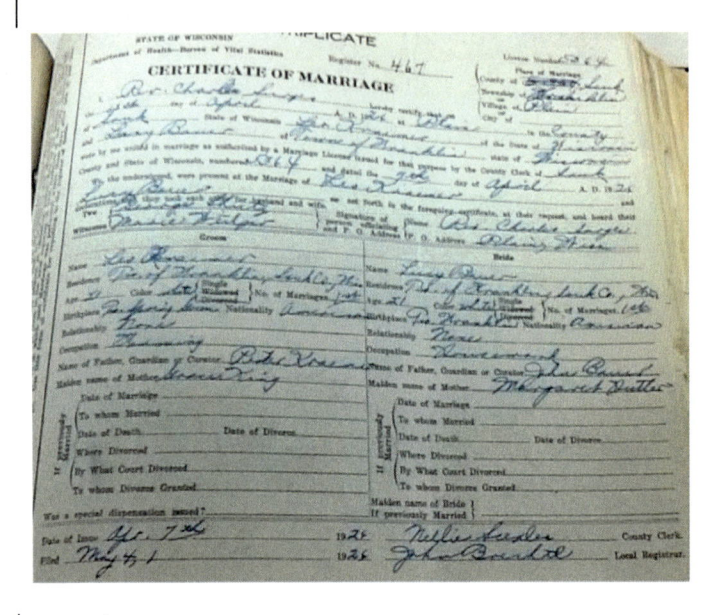

Place of marriage: Sauk County, Franklin Township, Village of Plain

State of Wisconsin, Department of Health

CERTIFIATE OF MARRIAGE

I, Rev. Charles Surges, hereby certify that on the 13th day of April A.D., 1926 at Plain in the County of Sauk, State of Wisconsin Leo Kraemer of the State of Wisconsin and Lucy Bauer of Town of Franklin, State of Wisconsin were by me united in marriage as authorized by a license issued for that purpose by the County Clerk of Sauk County and State of Wisconsin, numbered 5364 and dated the 7th day of April A.D., 1926. We the undersigned were present at the marriage of Leo Kraemer and Lucy Bauer at their request and heard their declarations as they took each other for husband and wife.

Two Witnesses:	George Schutz Marie Heiss	**Person Officiating:** Rev. Charles Surges Plain, Wis.
Groom: Leo Kraemer		**Bride:** Lucy Bauer
Residence: Twn of Franklin, Sauk Co.		Town of Franklin, Sauk Co.
Age: 21 Color: white, 1st marriage		21, white, 1st marriage
Birthplace: Twn Spring Green American		Town of Franklin, American
Relationship: None		None
Occupation: Farmer		Housework
Father: Peter Kraemer		John Bauer
Mother: Grace Ring		Margaret Hutter
Date of Issue: April 7th, 1924		Nellie Scexler, County Clerk
Filed: May 4, 1926		John Brechtl, Local Registrar

A neighbor lady helped my mother make the wedding dinner. There were few people at the wedding because I could not ask my brothers and sisters to the wedding and not also invite his brothers and sisters. And my mother couldn't afford such a large group.

The wedding was held at St. Luke's church. We had wedding pictures taken at Sauk City. The wedding dinner was held at my mother's home. After the dinner, we spent the day with the best man and bridesmaid. We went to a movie and then Leo took me to my home and he went to his home at Ted's. No shenanigans until the next day, "ha". The next day, dad came and got me, and we began our married life together.

Dad told me after 59 years that he didn't know if he really wanted to marry me at the time. He didn't explain what was on his mind. I said why didn't you tell me. I would have fixed it right away. He had already bought me a beautiful ring. I thought I really was somebody. But I didn't know what his thoughts were. So, we were married. [End of material from LUCY.]

RENTING OUR FIRST FARM

The day after we were married, we moved to Clem Frank's farm back in the pocket next to Ted's. We rented the farm for $800 a year. I could have bought the farm for $2,000 at one time but I didn't want it then. It had too much woods and too much fencing to maintain. I often wished that I had bought it afterwards.[7]

When I went farming, fieldwork was still done mainly with horses. There were no tractors. I had all good equipment and four beautiful horses. But I couldn't accumulate any money. One year the doctor bills and hired girl were $200 more than I took in. I milked nineteen cows. I could have bought a milk machine but

---

[7] When "Sunday driving" Leo and Lucy drove to that farm many times, talked about their life there and wished they had bought it. They even talked about buying it then. The children remember it well, including the emotions (sadness, wistfulness, regret, but also the happy, hopeful early days) that filled Leo and Lucy during those visits.

couldn't buy the gas engine to run it. We left the farm because Clem Frank wanted to get back into farming. He had tried being a butcher in town, but it didn't work out.[8]

Lucy, Leo, Virginia, circa, 1929

---

[8]Clem was married to Leo's sister Anna Kraemer. He later quit farming a second time and went to work for Ed Kraemer.

RENTING OUR SECOND FARM

In 1928, we rented the Rob Prouty farm [near White Mound where the George Schutz/Kenney Schutz farm is now located; see the map on p. 44].[9] We lived there three years renting the land, but we owned the livestock and equipment. We had two horses from the first farm. They were real wild and could jump a seven-foot fence. They never liked to stay around the barn. We always had to go up the hill to get them. When we left the Clem Frank farm we left the horses at Teds until we were ready to go to the Prouty farm. We left in January and stayed at dad's house in town until March when we went to the Prouty farm.

One time when we were loading hay into the hay loft, the hay was getting low on the wagon and the horse took off and ran. It got to the end of the rope and it threw him over backwards; he came back to where he was supposed to be and just stood there as if he'd been there all the time.

We had milk cows and raised pigs and chickens, but we could not make enough money to get ahead. When the depression hit in 1929, we really were hurting. The house and barn had been

---

[9] George bought the farm for $12,000.

built by Rob Prouty, but wasn't brand new. We usually slept downstairs in the house and mainly lived in the kitchen. We did washing outside by hand. We had a vegetable garden. Virgie was born on the Prouty farm. The farm was too much work for Lucy even though she was a hard worker. It was too much for me by myself, so we had to leave. When we sold everything, I got $420 less than I paid. I owed dad $3,000, which I had borrowed to set up the farm. [Leo never mentioned whether he paid back Pete.]

Leo, Virginia, Lucy and George Schutz, Jr. George bought the farm from Prouty after Leo and Lucy. Leo and George were close friends. They grew up on farms near one another, went to school together and spent teen years together.

Location of Leo Kraemer rented farms, Franklin Township, 1922

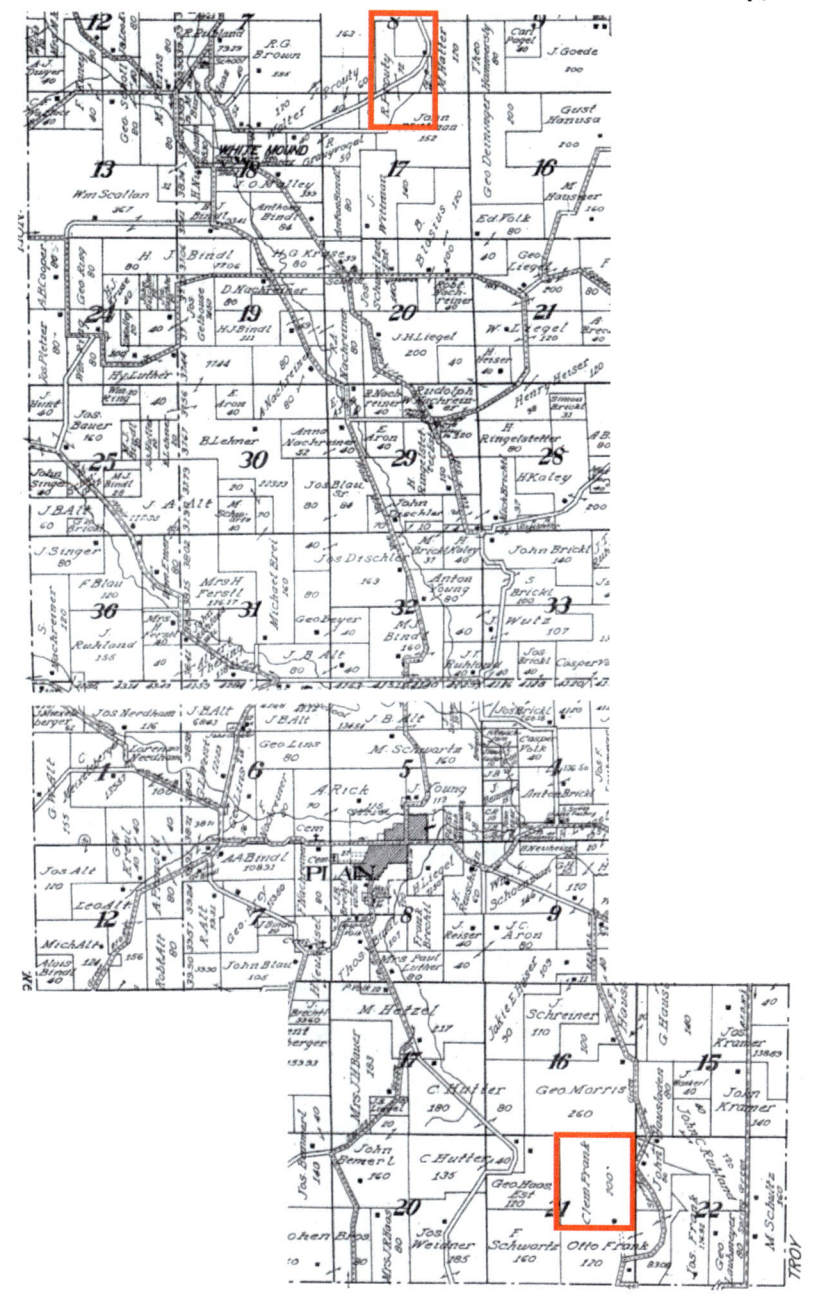

4. Work Life at EKS[10]

Ed [Kraemer; Leo's brother] had offered me a job, so we moved to town and I went to work for him. The first year I worked for Ed we loaded rock on trucks by hand. We would then haul the rock over to the crusher and dump it. County Highway B was the first road we built - from Highway 60 to the Harrisburg corner where C intersects B. We started there in January and finished about June. We then moved to Keysville and did the road thru Bear Valley down to the store. Then to Hillsboro and Yuba on Highway 80. They were all dirt roads at the time. Ed always did the work for less, so he always got the jobs. We didn't work when it rained, but we always went to work and then found out whether we would work. Jim Volk, Peter Plon and I would drive together. Jim had a model T.

I started work with Ed Kraemer in 1927 and worked for 44 years. [, Leo started work for EKS in 1929 at age 24 and worked 46 years to age 70 in 1975 according to EKS records, census records

---

[10] EKS stands for Edward Kraemer and Sons. Ed learned carpentry working for Bill Schwanke, a carpenter from Spring Green, who was building barns. At age 21, Ed built Georg Schutz's barn in Wilson Creek. Later, he lived in Lizzy Bettinger's house in the north half and built a house on Cedar Street for himself next to Post Heiser. Then he built the big stone house on Wachter Street near his shop and sold the other house to Mike Ring.

and the author's calculations].[11] I was twenty-six when I started working for them and seventy when I quit. There was only one road crew when I started. In a few years we went to three crews, and then we went to four. Then the boys [Ed's sons - Fred, Rudy and Victor] bought out Ed and got up to nine crews plus one each in Minneapolis, Ohio and Michigan.

I worked about 100+ quarries over the years. They ran from the upper end of the state (Hurley) to the lower end (Burlington), and from east (Green Bay) to the Mississippi (Onalaska) in the west. I worked in these places from about two to six weeks and usually lived in a bunk house except when the quarry was close to home. We all came home every night.

Shovel operator

When I first started working for Ed, we did everything by hand picking up rocks and throwing them on trucks which dumped them into the crusher. But we quickly got power equipment. I learned to run the shovel and Adam Soeldner ran the crusher. The service man from Northwest Power Shovels showed me how to run the shovel. I ran shovel for 14 years.

When I later became foreman, I had several shovel operators, but the chief one was Rennie Kraemer. Others were Barney Anders, Edwin Kraemer (son of John Kraemer), Ray Fleming and others I can't remember.

---

[11] George Soeldner worked for 50 years; he was eighteen when he started. He did bridge work and got to be foreman.

The shanty to the right in the photo on the next page might have been used for sleeping by the road crew. It was built in the shop and had solid rubber on steel rims and was hauled from quarry to quarry by a dump truck. The lettering on the side says: Edward Kraemer, Contractor, Plain, Wis.

The equipment in the photo below was from the 1930's. As Leo mentioned, the workmen picked up rocks by hand and loaded them on trucks which then backed on to the wooden platform (where the children are standing) and dumped the rocks into the large bin on the rock crusher. It was before Ed's sons became involved in the business and it became Edward Kraemer and Sons in the early 1940s. Ed started road building in 1927. Leo started work with Ed in 1929 – the beginning of the Great Depression.

Early crushing equipment

The trucks were first loaded by hand and later by power shovel as shown in the photo below. The men at the top are drillers preparing to dynamite the face of the quarry. More information about Edward Kraemer and Sons can be found in the excellent book by Claire Geesaman, *A Kraemer Chronicle*. Madison, WI: Edgewood College, 1992.]

Sources: unknown.

When the shovel was new (around 1929-30), we didn't have a trailer for moving it. We got a trailer from the County and used one truck in the front pulling and one in the back pushing to move it. We were down in Muscoda and had to go over by Blackhawk. We started Saturday and ran all day Saturday and Sunday; we ran all day Monday and that night into Tuesday. It took a total of thirty hours to move the shovel thirty miles, or about one mile and hour. The shovel didn't have metal tracks then; it had rubber. Every time you came to a wire (power or telephone pole) you had to crawl up the boom and move it over the boom and then crawl back into the cab to steer it.

    One time I started the shovel with the crank and it backfired and the crank went backwards and hit me on the arm and the ribs so hard that I couldn't run the shovel. Bill Miesie was the second shovel operator and he took over for me. We were on a hill and he pulled the clutch lever too hard and it snapped the drive chains and went down the hill backwards and rolled over three times until it hit bottom. We pulled it out with trucks and put it on a trailer. The cab was wrecked, the boom was off, and the engine was wrecked. We couldn't stop the job, so we rented a shovel from another contractor. We hauled the wrecked shovel back to the shop yard and the next winter Alphons and I rebuilt it in the shop [It probably involved welders, engine specialists and others as well.]

The first trailer we got for moving the shovel around had hard rubber tires and it cut through the ground whether dirt, gravel or blacktop. We had the trailer for six or seven years and then got a new one. We sold our shovel to a guy who came to pick it up in a trailer with air tires and we noticed that it didn't cut into the dirt or anything. I told Ed and he agreed to get a new trailer with air tires.

The move to foreman

I became foreman and began running the crusher after Adam Soeldner and did so for 22 years. I was forty when I went to running the crusher. I ran crusher and repaired them in the winter for the rest of my working life until retirement. The crushers were self-propelled, and you would drive them down the road. They could go about 20 miles an hour which was fast for a thing as big as that. I kicked one out of gear one time going down a hill; all at once it started picking up speed and I thought I would lose it. That was the last time I threw it out of gear. Towards the end of my work life, they had enough power in the engines to go up hills in high gear; they went from 250 to 800 horsepower. The same engine was used to drive the crusher as to crush rock.

The photo below shows the equipment used to produce gravel for roads. At the beginning was the power shovel. Rocks would have been blasted from the wall of the quarry the night before.

Drillers preparing to blast the quarry wall

The shovel was used to scoop up the rocks and put them into the mechanical breaker at the top of the first crushing unit. After going through the breaker, they were moved on a conveyer belt to a second crushing unit and another series of breakers that reduced them to the size needed for gravel. The crushed rock then entered a large hopper from which truck drivers would load the rock into their truck. The whole sequence of activity had to move at a synchronized pace so that there was enough rock in the hopper to fill each truck, while not having too much rock so that it ran over the hopper.

The worst job on a crushing crew was that of the "breaker man." This was a man who stood at the top of the crusher where the rock was deposited by the power shovel operated into a steel breaker. If some rocks were too large or jammed, it was his job to break them with a sledge hammer or wedge them apart with a long steel rod. It was a hot, noisy, dusty and dirty job that required the human breaker to stand on a narrow platform which was shaking from the force of steel plates banging against the rocks in the breaker.

There was the noise from the power shovel, the engine running the breaker, the breaker itself, the conveyer belts carrying rock from one breaker to another and the trucks entering and exiting the gravel hopper at the end of the process. There also might have been a bulldozer in operation pushing loose rocks into a pile so they would be easier for the shovel operator to load. The photo below is an enlargement showing the human breaker in position. The job was monotonous and it was easy for a breaker to get drowsy with danger of falling. Therefore the breaker had to be relieved every hour or so. The road crew foreman usually was the relief person for the "breaker man."

A "breaker man" in position on a rock crusher

Source: Edward Kraemer and Sons.

A rock-crushing unit

Source: Edward Kraemer and Sons.

The rock-crushing unit from above

Source: Edward Kraemer and Sons.

One time when I was working for the Town of Bear Creek I changed the roads from real steep up and down by cutting off the tops and filling in the valleys and taking the square corners and rounding them off. I cut off the hills and rounded corners all around the area - the Loretta Chapel, Alois Grubers, Needhams, etc. [12]

Life in the bunk house

The bunkhouse could accommodate 15-16 people and had an oil stove for heat. The men washed up with water from a dish pan; the water was usually carried from a local farmer's well in milk cans. In the evenings, some of the men would play cards. They would sit on the beds with two on each side of a suitcase or dynamite boxes. They played for pennies, sometimes for a nickel, and mainly played blackjack and poker. Other men would go to town; some chased women; some drank. Beer was ten cents a glass, which was too expensive for me. Some went to movies. We always had a cookhouse that went along with the road crew.

Mrs. Virgil Strait and Delores Kraemer were two of the cooks I remember. During the years that Reny Kraemer (son of John Kraemer of Iowa County) was my shovel operator,[13] the main cook was his wife Dolores Kraemer. Food was purchased daily from the local grocery stores located near the quarry. In some cases, it was purchased from farmers, e.g., eggs and vegetables, but mostly from stores.

---

[12] Roads originally followed property lines, which tended to be rectangular and required 90 degree turns. By rounding the corners, traffic would not have to stop at each turn. Roads also tended to follow natural contours. In the hilly country of southwestern Wisconsin, this meant a lot of ups and downs in the roads (which children loved). Cutting the hills and filling the valleys resulted in a more level road bed and smoother ride.

[13] During those years Leo and Reny would sit on the front porch on Sunday afternoons and talk swap stories about various jobs. That wonderful relationship changed when Reny become a foreman and they were now competing.

The Pulaski/Highway 29 job near Green Bay
One-day Rudy Kraemer brought Bobbie Liegel, my sister Lizzie's son, up to be a spotter. About noon one of Alois Hetzel's boys also came to be a spotter. I don't remember why but Bobbie Liegel was sent home rather than the Hetzel boy, but Bobbie was mad at me for sending him home.

Later you came and worked as spotter for a while.[14] Roger Ringlestetter also came and ran the water truck. He forgot how much the water sloshes around and tipped over the water truck and then he got sent home.

One week, we were short of men and you got to run the D9 Caterpillar bulldozer. I showed you how, but then you complained about how your arms and shoulders were hurting at the end of each day. I just thought you were not used to hard work. One day I took over and noticed that the gears were hard to operate. It turned out the Cat was short of hydraulic fluid.

We slept in the bunk house during the week and went home on weekends. Delores Kraemer was the cook and ran the cook house. Meals were good. She was a very good cook.

Work in the Shop
We usually worked in the shop from mid-December to early March because it was too cold and the ground too frozen to work on the roads. Our time was spent rebuilding, repairing and repainting crushing machines for the Spring season. There were two shop buildings tall enough for the machines, so we had to get four done during the 2-3-month period. There were several people who were always at the shop unless an emergency required them to come to a quarry.

Andy Soeldner was the shop foreman and chief mechanic.
Clem Ringelstetter ran the metal turning lathe.
Fred Schreiner was welder.
Alphonse Kraemer did carpenter work.

---

[14] A spotter stood with a flag on a pole indicating how far each gravel truck was to back up before unloading their gravel on the road bed. Some drivers did a quick release to partially bury the spotter as a joke.

When we came into the shop these guys would help us with rebuilding the machines. They would teach us how to run some of the equipment and help us with the difficult tasks or when special skill was required. When necessary, we helped them, e.g., build (or rebuild) a sleep shanty or cook house.

Leo and Lucy, circa 1945

We didn't make much money

Even though it was bad at times, I was glad to have a job. We didn't get paid much and everything was hourly. In the late forty's or early fifties, the State got involved and set the wages that had to be paid, so we got more money then.

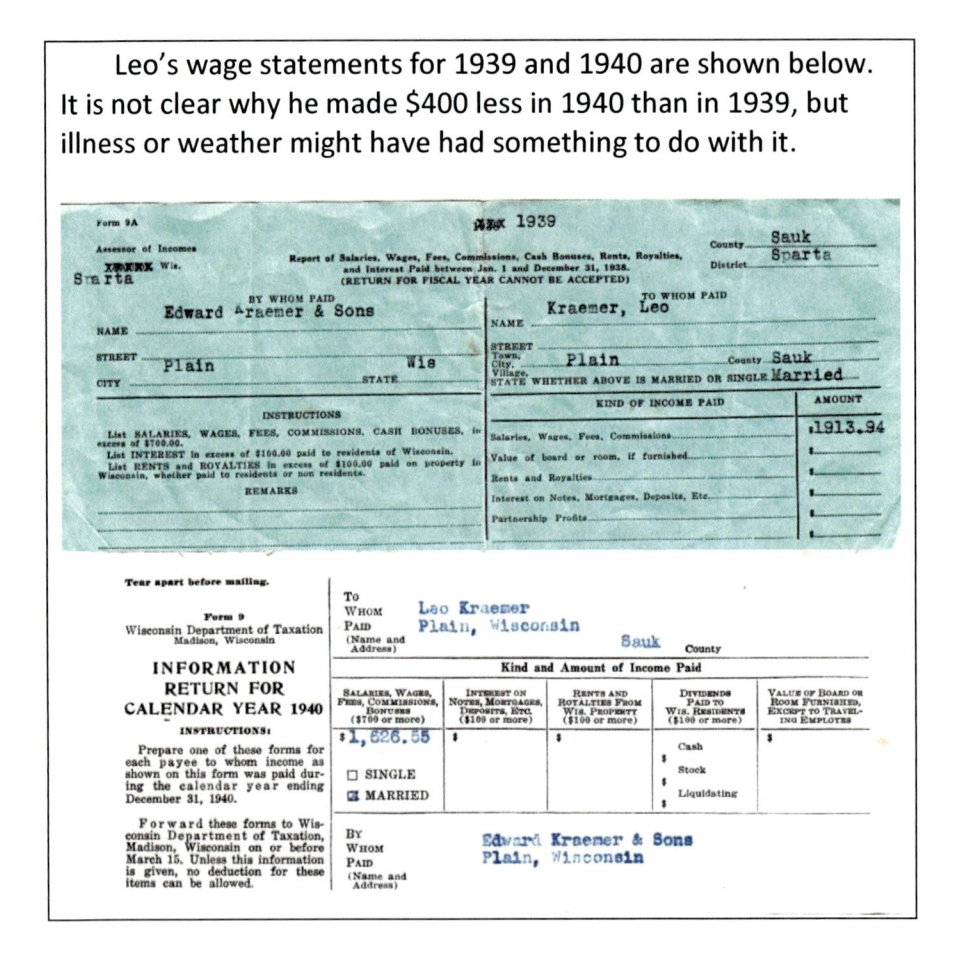

> Leo's wage statements for 1939 and 1940 are shown below. It is not clear why he made $400 less in 1940 than in 1939, but illness or weather might have had something to do with it.

[1939 wage statement: Edward Kraemer & Sons, Plain, Wis., paid to Kraemer, Leo, Plain, Sauk County, Married — Amount: $1913.94]

[1940 Information Return, Wisconsin Department of Taxation: Paid to Leo Kraemer, Plain, Wisconsin, Sauk County — Salaries, Wages, Fees, Commissions, Bonuses: $1,526.55, Married — By Whom Paid: Edward Kraemer & Sons, Plain, Wisconsin]

Today there is very scientific blasting. There are very few boulders. If there are any, they move them aside with a skip loader and then break them with a ball on a crane or blast them later. They use very large drills like a well drill and simply drill down and put the dynamite at different levels. They don't have to drill at the bottom anymore.

How I felt about work

I always enjoyed moving from place to place. When I was younger I moved from farm to farm. I worked two years at Teds. Then I worked 7 months at Frank's farm and went to Ben's farm in the winter. I worked three months for Ed in the carpenter business. The I worked another 2-3 years for Ted after that. Later, when I worked for Ed on road construction, I moved from quarry to quarry. It was interesting to see the different quarries and the different conditions.

Ed would visit the quarries on a regular basis. He always came with the dog. [Dad did not remember him coming with Duane or with any of his boys. Only the dog.] Later the boys took over and Rudy or Vic would visit the quarries. They took turns and did not divide up the quarries between them.

> Leo doesn't mention it directly, but he felt a lot of stress in his job. Ren Kraemer [another foreman] and dad would occasionally sit on the front porch steps on Sundays and talk about the jobs they were working on and how they were being pushed for more production from their crews. Vic and Rudy would compare production statistics between quarries and ask each foreman why they couldn't do as well as another foreman. There was great variation between quarries and between jobs which Vic and Rudy didn't always consider.

Vic Kraemer put me into a quarry in Menomonie, WI that had as much dirt as rock. Ren had been there and somehow got them to move him home. It was the middle of winter and the clay and rock would freeze up. It was difficult.

Work injuries

I lost part of my forefinger though a work accident. One of the trucks would not start so we got the bulldozer to pull it. I was looking at how the chain had been connected and was sticking my finger in a hole when one of the drillers pulled the chain with a jerk and cut it off. I didn't even notice it at first, but when I did I was so shocked I almost fainted. I wrapped a rag around it and went to the doctor. I went back to work right away. It was very sensitive for a while.

    I broke my wrist while working as the "breaker man" on the crusher. I was jamming a long steel bar in the crusher to break some rocks and the bar got caught and started swinging back and forth. The bar hit my wrist and broke it all the way around. I went to a doctor in Green Bay and had a cast put on it. It took six weeks to heal.

5. CHILDREN

Lucy and I had three girls and three boys. Until Ken came along, I thought we would have all girls.

Virgie was born on February 28, 1928 while we were still on the Prouty farm.

Leo, Virgie and Lucy, circa 1930

I took Lucy to Heiss's [Marie Heiss, in Madison] a week before the baby was born and I went to Green Bay. Lucy's mother [Margaret Bauer] kept Virgie. It was really snowing. The road was lower than the fields, so people drove through the fields to Arena. By the time I came home there was no snow on the road. I was in Green Bay when Doris was born at St. Mary's hospital in Madison. We lived in the little house in Plain at the time.

[The photo below shows Virgie and Doris, Lucy's homemade chair, the outdoor toilet and garden shed. Gruber's tavern is just behind them, and Daniel Ruhland's house and Diehl's tavern are in the background and across the street from Gruber's tavern.]

Doris and Virgie

Photo shows backyard of little house with shed and outdoor toilet. Gruber's tavern and outdoor toilet are directly behind.

Three years later Phyllis was born (1933). I took mother to St. Mary's hospital in the morning and left right away for work. Carrie Hauslauden, who was Ferry Hauslauden's daughter, took care of Virgie and Doris. [Carrie's grandmother was Frances Weidner]. I came the next day to see how things were and Phyllis was already born at 11pm the night before. We were still living in the little house.

Doris, Virgie (holding Ken), Phyllis, circa 1936

The building in the background is probably Joe Frank's barn.

In between having Phyllis and Ken, we bought our first house in 1934. The house had been owned by Frank Martin who worked at the bank in Plain. Ed had loaned the money for the house to Frank. He was married to Emma Frank who was the sister of Ed's wife Gisela Frank. When the bank when bankrupt, the Martin's moved to Baraboo. Ed then sold the house to us.[15] The house cost $2200. The note (below) was for four percent interest annually until paid, but Ed never took the interest when we paid it off in 1941. We kept a record of our payments on small sheet of paper (see below). We paid about $50 every couple of months and sometimes more when we could. We were anxious to pay off the loan. We didn't like being in debt to anyone.

---

[15] John W. Bauer, who was related to the Dischlers, had built the house. Eleven different people had owned the land before us. John Bauer was Mrs. Clem Luther's father. He owned the Joseph Kraemer's house at one time and built mother and dad's house [next door to Joseph]. Mary Bauer was J.W.'s daughter. She and Esther were classmates. I came to the house once with Ester and there used to be a porch all along the back of the house. Mary Bauer married Pete Kessnick of Bear Valley.

Original note for the house loan, 1934

$2200.00   PLAIN, WIS., November 28, 1934

November 28, 1937   AFTER DATE, FOR VALUE RECEIVED, I OR WE PROMISE TO PAY

Edward Kraemer _____ OR ORDER, AT

THE PLAIN STATE BANK
IN PLAIN, WISCONSIN

Twentytwo Hundred and no/100----------------------------- DOLLARS

WITH INTEREST AFTER DATE, AT THE RATE OF Four PER CENT PER ANNUM, UNTIL PAID.

Leo A Kraemer
Lucy Kraemer

Record sheet for paying off the loan, 1935-1941

Note: "Red on principl" means Reduction on principal.

Red on principl	2-16-35	$50.00	
" " "	4-18-"	50.00	
" " "	6-4-"	75.00	
" " "	8-4-"	75.00	
" " "	9-22-"	75.00	
" " "	11-19-"	75.00	
" " "	1-2-36	50.00	
" " "	3-3-36	50.00	
" " "	6-7-36	75.00	
" " "	8-19-36	100.00	
" " "	12-7-36	40.00	71.5
" " "	7-5-37	100.00	
" " "	8-9-37	75.00	175
" " "	11-20-38	50.00	50
" " "	5-29-39	100.00	
" " "	9-4-39	100.00	
" " "	7-10-39	100.00	50
" " "	10-4-39	200.00	

Total payments to 12/31/39   1,440.00
Bal Due 1/1/40   760.00
Red on principl 12-15-40   50.00
Bal Due 12/31/40   710.00
Red on principl 6-1-41   200.00
"   "   "   10-5-41   510.00

Pd in full

House at Cedar Street and Park Avenue

Photo by Gary Haas. House on Park Ave. at Cedar St., Plain, WI.

When we moved to the house in November, I was working out on the road. Lucy had to get people to help her. [Lucy recalled the following about the move:] *Johnny my brother and Veronica* [daughter of Joseph Kraemer and a housekeeper] *moved us. There was snow on the ground and he moved us with a wagon and horses. Veronica and I carried all three beds, mattresses and bedclothes up the stairs. We had no dressers, except one for the bedroom and the bed to match it that mother gave to me. Leo had a big trunk, which you must remember that was on the upstairs landing, where the cupboard now is across the landing. We also had a table and chairs Leo moved the stove on a Sunday when he had someone to help him. Frank Martin wanted to take out the hot water heater and someone told him everything bolted to the floor could not be taken out. It was connected to the kitchen stove. We had to heat cooking kettles of water and carry it upstairs when we took a bath.*

Virgie, "Spike" Lucy, Doris and playhouse

L>R: Virginia, "Spike" (Veronica Kraemer's dog), Lucy and Doris Kraemer. Note the play house on the right and the home-made chair. Alphons Kraemer house is in background.

You [Ken] were born in the house [Cedar St.]. Fowler and Liz [the midwife, Elizabeth Bettinger] delivered the baby. I sat at the dining room table. I looked in occasionally and the doctor said, "You get out of here!" One half hour after you were born, I went to work. You had to go to work. I was somewhere close by because I came home at night. The kids [Virgie, Doris, Phyllis] went to Annie's [Leo's sister] because they were driving mother nuts.

You had a lot of trouble. They couldn't get you to cry. You were a breach birth, born with the cord around your neck. You looked like a tiger, stripped with blue/purple stripes. I asked Liz Bettinger if it would go away. Liz cared for you at her house after you were born. She put you in a shoebox in the oven to keep you warm [incubator].

When Lucy was pregnant with Jan, she had to go to the hospital to have her appendix taken out. Jan was born at Liz Bettinger's. I was working at Platteville. A hired girl was helping Lucy with the kids. Lucy walked over to Liz Bettinger's house and said, "This is it" and she called Dr. Fowler. I came home the following Saturday and saw. Jan had "rickets" when he was little, but got over them with extra Vitamin D.

Leo & Lucy's family, circa 1937

L>R: Leo, Lucy holding Kenneth (baby), Virginia, Phyllis, Doris. Where this photo was taken is unclear.

1942 was the year Ron was born. He also was born at Liz Bettinger's house with Dr. Fowler. Coletta Lins was taking care of the kids when Ron was born. Mom let Ron's hair grow long like a girl. [See earlier photo in Chapter 2 of Leo with long hair as a child.]

The boys, circa, 1942

L>R: Ronald, Kenneth and Jan Kraemer (Irwin Kruse's dog).

Leo Kraemer children, circa 1950

Row 1, L>R: Jan, Ronald and Ken; Row 2: L>R: Doris, Phyllis and Virginia Kraemer

Map of Plain with house locations

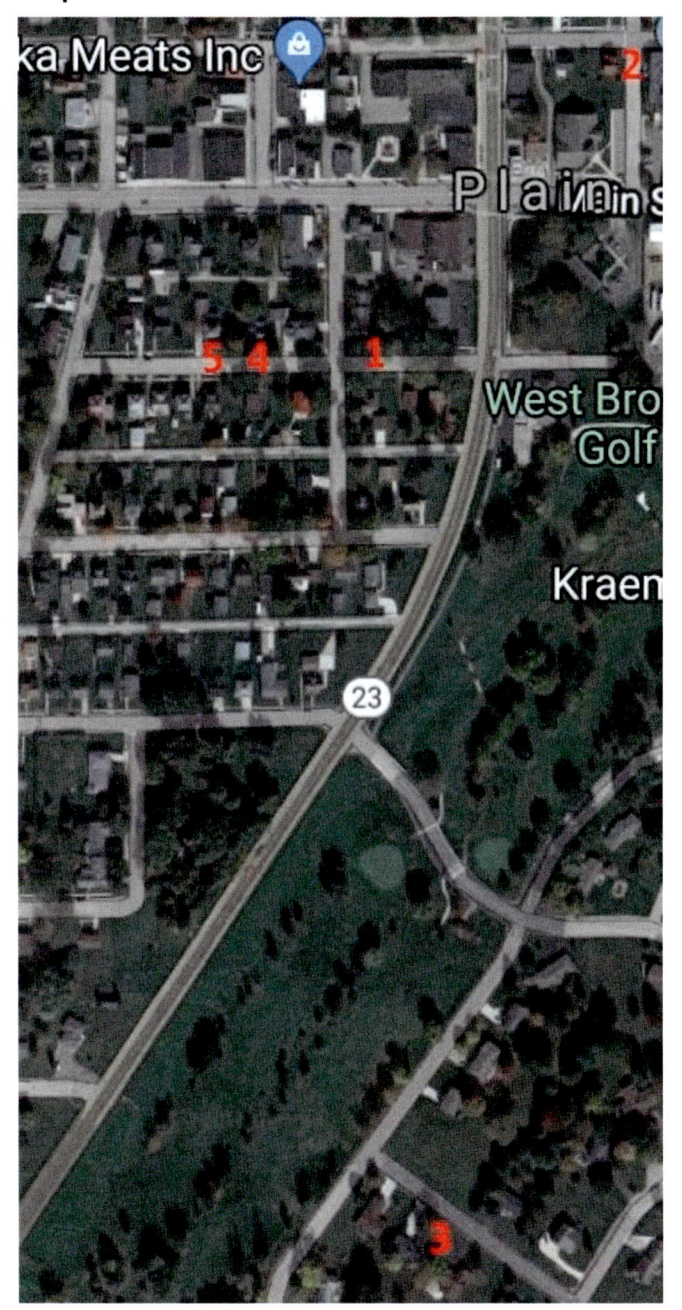

Legend:
1 = Small rental house on Liegel St. and Clover Ave.
2 = First home on Cedar St. and Park Ave.
3 = Final home in Westbrook
4 = Peter and Katharine
5 = Joseph, Theresia and Veronica Kraemer

We had lots of hired girls to help out mother. At the Prouty farm we had Marie Heiss, Ruth Neiman, Mary Dietl and John Blau's daughter. At the little house, we had Lucy Dischler and Carrie Hauslauden. At our house on Cedar St., we had Colleta Lins and Veronica Kraemer.

Veronica came to help with the washing and ironing once a week. It was easy to get somebody in those days.

Leo Kraemer family, circa 1986

Row 1, L>R: Phyllis, Doris; Row 2, L>R: Leo, Lucy, Jan; Row 3, L>R: Ron, Virginia, Ken

Leo Kraemer children, 2008

L>R: Ronald, Virginia, Phyllis, Doris, Kenneth, Jan. Photo by Norine Kraemer.

6. WEDDINGS

Leo did not speak about the weddings of his children, so we include Lucy's account in his stead. This entire chapter is from the book, *LUCY* (2015).

Virgie and Ray

When we heard about Virgie's wedding, I had to get busy and pick chickens. An old lovely lady named Lena Reaser (God Bless Her) helped me and we picked 70 chickens. I couldn't cut the heads, so I asked her to do it. When I was young and asked to kill chickens, I stepped on the heads and quickly pulled the heads off. Now I shiver when I think of it.

Virgie and Doris went for the wedding cake. …We had 90 for dinner and one hundred eighty-five for reception. The bride's maids had brocaded yellow and pink dresses the girls made themselves. They were brocaded organdy. The flower girl had blue organdy also made by Doris. Virginia had her dress made by Mrs. Herman Blau, a dressmaker.

When Leo walked into the dining room the night before the wedding, he said it really looks beautiful. He had been at work and did not see it until the night before.

After living in Plain for several years, Virgie, Ray and their son Mike moved to a small mining town in Minnesota. I could see how they were accepted by the people, growing closer each time. I coaxed Phyllis to visit Virginia. She did and got a job and they took

part in the church and it wasn't long and Cohasset built a beautiful church.
Virgie and Ray, 1951

L>R: Unknown, Ken, Ray Fleming, Virginia, Doris and Phyllis Kraemer.

As they were moving, we got an education in traveling. Every Spring and fall, Cohasset had the visiting Kraemer's. We went to dances, fishing, meeting their neighbors. Ray Fleming was employed by the mines and later by the power and light company until his retirement. The eldest daughter [Virgie] of the Kraemers works for DNR. The second daughter [Doris] is postmaster at Plain. The third [Phyllis] is secretary to Principal of Cohasset elementary school. Granddaughter Julie is in forestry. John Fleming graduated in optometry in California, married a Californian, and moved to Minnesota. Michael Fleming moved to California, married in California and is installing security systems there. Neil Fleming is employed with a large oil plant in Alaska and likes it. Gene Fleming was in the service at Great Lakes until he got an illness and was discharged. He is now a bartender.

Doris and Vernon

Virginia and Doris's wedding were only four months apart, so it really kept me busy [maybe it seemed like only four months]. When Doris heard that Vernon was coming home on a furlough and would be transferred to Washington D.C., they planned a wedding on December 27, 1952. Then they would go there to live. Then I never dreamed that I was to go there someday.

When she got there Doris got sick again and was to have an operation for bleeding polyps at Walter Reed hospital. Leo couldn't go along. So, Kenneth took me to Spring Green train station. I left for Madison to pick up my reservations at Chicago to Washington D.C. When I got to Chicago there wasn't a soul in the depot; they had all gone to the train. The Information Desk gave me a reservation and I was to go on Door 5. I finally, after walking along five train cars, saw someone who said to go three more cars and when I got there a Negro picked up my suitcase and the train left. I sat down and cried and cried. Finally, a man sat by me and tried to console me.

When I was in Washington D.C. visiting Doris and Vernon, Vernon decides to take me for a tour around Washington. We went to the Washington Monument, the White House (we didn't go inside the White House), then Lincoln Memorial, to Arlington Cemetery Tomb of the Unknown Soldier, the cherry blossoms were *in full bloom, all the flowers were just beautiful. Next, he took me to the park, and, when he locked his keys inside the door, he walked back home.*

Doris and Vernon Bindl, 1952

Standing, L>R: Vernon Bindl, Doris Kraemer, George Liegel, Delbert Schutz, Kenneth Kraemer. Sitting, L>R: Donelda Bindl, Phyllis Kraemer, Norine Bindl.

He got a ride part of the way, and while he got the ride, he heard on the radio, that a man swiped a woman's purse and hit her over the head at the park. So, Vernon thought, Oh God, what if it was Lucy. But it wasn't me; I followed the crowd; if they went to the snakes, I went to the snakes. When he got back he took me to see the birds. I was plenty scared going to the hospital every day, and it was my luck that I was the only one in the taxi, both ways.

Phyllis and Jim

Now we come to the third daughter and that was a problem. She did not care to go dance; she couldn't find anyone of interest to her. She would much rather drag a step ladder and all the paints all the way up to Saint Ann's Hill to paint the Stations of the Cross. One time she was sent over to Father Beschta with seven boys. When they got in there Father said, "Well now Phyllis, I just can't believe that." She was a menace to the class and disturbed the class. He just sent them all back to school.

When Phyllis graduated from high school, Doris was working at the powder plant near Baraboo, and she finally talked Phyllis into going to work with her. After Doris got married and went to Washington D.C. with Vernon, I talked Phyllis into making a visit to our oldest daughter Virgie, who had moved to Cohasset Minnesota. I had to talk pretty fast but I made it.

In three weeks she turned up with a converted Norwegian with a crew cut. It was the first crew cut I saw. I brushed my hand over his head to see if it was real. I had promised her she might find a nice boyfriend and she did. She had an all-white wedding. Bride's maid had white hats and, so I had a good job finding white wire and making a frame for the hats. I really don't know where I got the wire for three hats. The girls put on the brocaded veil that was mostly Doris's job. The hats were beautiful.

When Phyllis got married in 1955, Leo was in the hospital for a pinched nerve in his neck. Dr. Fowler let him come home that morning. Marie Heiss [Lucy's niece who lived in Madison] *picked him up. He walked Phyllis up the aisle, ate a light dinner, and they took him back to the hospital and put him back in traction again. I think that is giving him trouble now again.*

Phyllis and Jim Avenson, 1955

L>R: Doris Pronold, Donelda Bindl, Elsie Ruhland, Phyllis Kraemer, James Avenson, Kenneth Kraemer, Robert Kraemer, Eugene Alt.

It was time for a check-up for Leo. Dr. Garlarnyk found polyps, which he removed; but there was one that he couldn't reach so they had to operate again, and it was cancerous; no problems since.

When Leo was in the hospital, I would take the bus from Spring Green to the bus station in Madison. Then take a bus to St. Mary's. I would go to the hospital in the morning about 9 o'clock and go back to Marie Heiss's at night at 8 o'clock. One-night rain just poured down. I had to take a cab from the "square" in Madison. When I did get a cab, he talked so much, and I got scared and was glad when we finally got to Marie's. No one else was in the cab. Now when I think back I can't believe that I did that. It was no problem for me to go to the Capital and straight through to the other side. One time the bus driver forgot to call when he got to Mifflin St., so I knew he forgot and I told him, and he gave me a transfer slip and I had to change to a bus going back 3 blocks. There I had to go through a school playground over to Roger's Memorial Hospital.

Ken and Norine Wedding

I can't tell you much about this because we only furnished the drinks and it was in 1959. You can add the rest. No one believed our three boys were in the wedding. It was such fun because I didn't have to do any planning. Ask Norine to fill in her wedding.

Kenneth graduated from St. Luke's in Plain, was awarded the degree, Bachelor of Architecture of Notre Dame at the 115 Commencement Exercise Sunday, June 7. He was commissioned second lieutenant in the Air Force at class day exercises where he also received the Kervick Medal for excellence in architecture. He was also married to Norine Bindl in 1959. But Leo could not take off work so Doris drove the car and we had a lovely time at the graduation. Graduation was at the college football stadium. It was beautiful, and we stayed overnight and Doris, Norine and I left the next day. Later the same year Norine and Kenneth left for March Air Force base where they made their home for 18 months.

Ken and Norine, 1959

L>R: Vernon Bindl, Ron Kraemer, Doris Jean Bindl, Richard Novy, Ken Kraemer, Norine Bindl, Donelda (Bindl)Novy, Suzy Prem, Jan Kraemer, Melvin Weiss.

While Kenneth was still going to Notre Dame, my sister-in-law told me he was growing away from us. Then I didn't think much about it but as time went on I realized that if you hadn't proceeded with your education I never would have seen your graduation, that Alvina and I never would have seen the nice trip on the train to California and Disneyland. On our 45th wedding anniversary Leo and I went to California to visit Ken and Norine and saw Disneyland. We had a helicopter ride to Riverside. That was a terrific experience, which I would never want to repeat.

Jan and Colleen

We couldn't decide if we should go to the wedding. Leo was working, and he sure must have liked his job. I did buy a black dress; the top was lace and a short bolero over the lace top. How I would have liked it if Leo has said we would go. [The wedding was in Anaheim, CA, where Coleen's family lived. Mom and dad and others were unable to make it. Norine and I lived nearby in Orange, CA, attended the wedding on the Kraemer side.]

Ron and Kathy

The night before Ron and Kathy's wedding we had a cloudburst. Water was so high that they were rowing boats down behind our house. Mary Dischler came over and said let's go down in the water and walk. The water came up to our garage, and as we got going it came up to our knees. Tim Walsh came along. He said do you want a ride, and we said yes, and got in. A whiskey bottle was floating around in the car. It was fun but when Tim started moving the car forward it stalled and he couldn't get it going again, so we got out and walked up to the filling station.

I was worried that I was going to have the cramps, so I took a bath and went to bed. But everything went fine. We left the next morning and stayed at the Bauer house overnight. It was a beautiful wedding. Our girls who were living in Cohasset came also. There was lots of food. And the next morning we left for home leaving our baby boy with his bride. We also met lots of nice people.

Jan and Colleen Riffle, 1963

L>R: Tim Walsh, Noreen Riffle, Coleen Riffle, Jan Kraemer, Roger Ringelstetter, Ken Kraemer

Ron Kraemer and Kathy Bauer, 1965

L>R: Cathy Bauer, Ron Kraemer, Tim Walsh, unknown.

7. RETIREMENT

I retired in 1975 at age 70. I had worked forty years for Edward Kraemer and Sons, mostly out on the road rather than in the shop.

After retirement, I would sometimes go down to the shop to see some of the men I worked with, but after a while I didn't know the new people anymore, so I stopped going.

In 1977-78, I helped Vernon [Bindl; son-in-law] with work on the Bindl family farm. I did plowing and disking, silo filling, haying, picking corn, building a hog house, sorting pigs for sale, and butchering pigs (Documented in Alvina Bindl diaries, 1975-1979).

I made sauerkraut in a 30-gallon stone crock. Later in the year, I made wine in the same crock – some from wild grapes and some from store grapes.

I walked a lot, usually every day except in the winter. I would go south on County B out of town and back. I golfed with Doris, Vernon, Father McAleer and others. I also played golf by myself.

When Lucy could not do it anymore, I made meals and took care of her flowers around the house. I also did the laundry and house cleaning.

Leo tending Lucy's flowers

Wedding Anniversaries

We lived a long time, so Lucy and I had a lot of wedding anniversaries. We celebrated 50th, 60th and 70th anniversaries. As we passed 70 years, we made the paper almost every year. I guess they thought we might not be around the next year on our anniversary.

Our big anniversary was the 50th in 1976. It was the same year as the 200th anniversary of the Declaration of Independence.

Lucy was all dolled up for the reception and people came from everywhere – including our best man and bride's maid.

50th wedding anniversary, 1976, Palace Hall

[After, the 50th celebration, Marie Heiss, who had been the maid of honor in 1926 and was present, wrote a letter to Phyllis:

Dear Phyllis and Jim,
It was a beautiful party you all put on for your parents and how lucky I was to be part of it. So many people came to me and said, "Hi Marie" and I had to ask whom they were. Even Sep's girls and Francis Bauer I didn't recognize. I enjoyed it as did my family. …But what I really enjoyed was the Mass. Tell Mark he did a beautiful job as did Jan's daughter. Weren't the little ones' darling who brought up the wine and water, etc. …It really made up for your mom's wedding day although at that time I thought it too was beautiful. …Also for her dear friend Leona Butler to be there really pleased her.
Love, Marie (Heiss)

[Marie's remark that *"it really made up for your mom's wedding day..."* was referring to the fact that the 1926 wedding had only 14 people because that was all that Lucy's mother could afford. Neither Lucy's brothers and sisters nor Leo's could be invited.]

Leo and Lucy, George Schutz and Marie Heiss, 1926 and 1976

1926 photo, L>R: Leo, Lucy, George Schutz, Marie Heiss:
1976 photo, L>R: George Schutz, Marie Heiss, Lucy and Leo.

For the 60th, we had an open house at the Palace Hall. It was announced in the *Home News* along with our picture (below).

Kraemers observe 60th anniversary, 1986

Leo and Lucy Kraemer will celebrate their 60th wedding anniversary on Sunday, July 6. Open house will be held at the Palace Hall, Plain, from 2 to 5pm. No gifts please. Weekly Home News, July 1986.

The following story was in the Home News for the 71st anniversary.

Kraemers celerate 71st , April 13, 1997

Lucy Bauer and Leo Kraemer were married on April 13, 1926 at St. Luke's Catholic Church in Plain. Leo worked for Edward Kraemer and Sons until his retirement in 1975 at age 70, while Lucy stayed home to raise their six children, Virginia Fleming, Spring Green, Doris Bindl and Jan, Plain; Phyllis Avenson, Cohasset, Minnesota; Kenneth, Irvine, California and Ron, San Diego, California. The couple has 25 grandchildren and 25 great-grandchildren.

By age 75, Leo was finding retirement somewhat uneventful and his wife's health was declining so he decided to try his hand at golf, baking, cooking, cleaning and laundry, discovering he was pretty competent at all of it.

In 1996, the couple moved from their home of 63 years to a newer, more convenient one, enabling Leo to continue cring for Lucy.

Lucy, Leo and Rev. Mike Resop, 71th anniversary

Source: *Home News*, April 16, 1997, page 9

Visiting children

Almost every year, we went to northern Minnesota to visit daughters Virginia Fleming and Phyllis Avenson, and to Minneapolis to visit son Ron. We were always kept busy running around with the different families. I did a lot of fishing with Ray Fleming in Cohasset.

Laundry in Cohasset

Out on the town

Playing cards

Chris and David Avenson, Leo and Lucy

Leo celebrates his sisters' birthdays

L>R: Anna (Frank), Leo and Elizabeth (Liegel) Kraemer.

Westbrook, Greenway Manor, The Meadows

[In 1996, Leo and Lucy moved to a new place in Westbrook area of Plain to a house that was one story. Lucy had developed dementia and dad was afraid of her falling down stairs either from the second story or to the basement of the old house. It helped, but Leo could not get sleep as Lucy would roam the house during the night and sometimes get outside. His own health was failing too and so sometime in 1998, Lucy went to the Greenway Manor Nursing Home in Spring Green. [

[Earlier, when speaking about his teens, Leo had said: "I liked to dance but I was afraid to go out on the dance floor because I was always concerned that I was not as good as the others." It looks like he overcame that fear in his old age.]

At the Meadows   **With Chris Avenson**

Source: Doris Bindl.

Leo at The Meadows

As Lucy's dementia developed, she tended to fall into a staring, trance-like look as the photos below show. Dad was living at The Meadows at the time as there was no assisted living at Greenway. Lucy became more and more confused as time when on, but Dad's presence usually helped as did that of Doris and Jan and other family members who visited.

Lucy at Greenway Manor

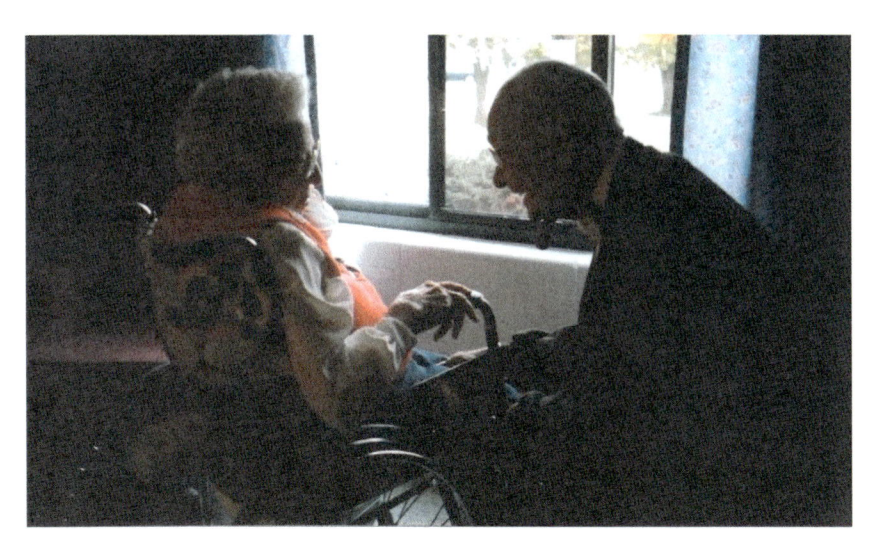

Favorite prayer: The Rosary.

Regrets
Leo had a few regrets about missed opportunities in his life. He said:
I regret not buying the farm by Ted's" and *"I regret not going into [road] business with Louie Meise.* I noted elsewhere that Kraemers were characterized by an entrepreneurial spirit and it appears Leo was no exception. No doubt the Depression and Lucy's many illnesses influenced the former; we know nothing about his opportunity to go into the road business with Louie Meise.

Self-description
*I was a loner. I had nobody to play with when I was young. I didn't do things with girls when I was a teenager. I liked to dance but I was afraid to go out on the dance floor because I was always concerned that I was not as good as the others. My dad thought I was too small to do much work. I kept trying to compete with my older brothers Frank and Ben to prove him wro*ng [Telephone conversation with Leo, 1999].

Postscript

The above is the end of dad's story telling. The rest of this book is built from other letters, research and my recollections.

Lucy died at 96, October 7, 2000 at Greenway Manor in Spring Green. Please see her story in *LUCY*, 2015.

Leo died two years later April 15, 2002 at the age of 97[16] at The Meadows assisted living in Spring Green. He was buried next to Lucy at St. Luke's cemetery in Plain. The family posted the following "Thanks" in the *Home News* after his funeral.

The Family of Leo Kraemer

Wishes to express their sincere thanks to Father Mike Resop, Father John Auby, Sister Helene, the Richardson-Stafford Funeral Home, the ladies of Lt. Luke's Circles who served the meal, relatives and friends who brought food, for all the prayers, flowers and memorials. A special thanks to the staff of "The Meadows" where Dad made his home for four years, for the kind and thoughtful care they gave him, to all his friends living there who made him feel welcome and at home. Your kindness and sharing made him feel accepted and happy. He truly felt it to be "home."

Dad died at The Meadows, April 15, 2002, 9:15pm, Ken's account

Dad went into the Sauk Hospital for blood transfusions and tests and then went to the Greenway Manor nursing home following his last blood transfusion. Dad had multiple problems at the time of death: pneumonia, thyroid failure, liver failure, congestive heart failure and swelling in his toes and feet from poor blood circulation. He was too old and close to death to do anything about the circulation problem and so his feet kept getting worse and worse.

---

[16] Lucy was a year older than Leo having been born in 1904 and he in 1905.

When Dad realized he was at Greenway, he asked to be moved because he wanted to die at the Meadows. He requested that he be moved there because he knew the people and had come to like them. Doris went through a lot of effort and got him moved. From the time he moved into the Meadows until he died (only two days) he was very uncomfortable and did not seem to be able to get comfortable. He had stomach problems. He would throw-up his food if he ate. He did eat some "smorn"with apple sauce that Virgie made for him and he kept it down.

He had trouble breathing when he laid down and therefore always wanted to sit up; yet he got very tired when he did so and sometimes lost his balance sitting up. Throughout the day of his death, he would sit up, lay down and then want to sit up again. We moved him up and down around 50 times during that day. He did not eat at all and could not even drink water. He took water on a sponge and ice chips. We were able to get him to take Tylenol with applesauce on a tea spoon about 7:30pm and thought that he would then go to sleep. Although he tried to lay down, he could not stay that way. When we refused to help him get up (thinking he needed to sleep), he simply started to get up on his own and then we helped him so that he would not fall out of bed.

He had fallen out the day before after we had laid him down and he had gone to sleep. Apparently, he woke up, had trouble breathing and tried to get up by himself. He lost his balance and was kneeling on the floor saying, "Help me, help me..." when Phyllis and I found him after talking a walk around the Meadows parking lot for some air.

Phyllis and Virgie went to Virgie's for dinner around 7:30pm. I stayed because I was not hungry and because Sandy [a patient care-giver] asked if one of us could stay a little longer until she finished working with the other residents. Then she was going to give dad a bath and put him to bed. The time kept getting postponed. Around 8:30pm Sandy (Heiser) tried to talk him into going to sleep by saying over and over, "Leo you are not alone. We will be here when you wake up in the morning. Your family will be here in the morning." It seemed to be working, but then he wanted to be up again. About 8:45pm, Phyllis and Virgie came back from dinner and I went back to Virgie's to have dinner. They came home about 9:00 and we were called by Sandy about five minutes later. We got to the Meadows about 9:15pm and he had already taken his last breadth. His eyes were still open and there was slight movement around his mouth. In less than a minute his eyes closed on their own. Virgie kissed him on the forehead and said something to him. Phyllis did too. We held his hand and said, "We love you dad."

    Doris and Vernon and then Coleen and Jan appeared shortly thereafter. I don't remember what they did. We cried and held one another. Jan was particularly upset. I sat in the wheel chair and just looked at dad. He seemed at rest for the first time since I had seen him at Greenway Manor the week before—it was the rest that I was hoping he would get all day Monday, but it wasn't rest. He was dead.

    Wilma was the person who was with dad when he died. She had laid him down just before Phyllis and Virgie left for the night and then gone on to check the blood pressure of another resident. When she got back, dad's condition had made a marked shift and it was clear that he was dying from his breathing. They called us immediately and we went immediately.

    We had no idea that he was really dying so soon. He did not seem to be in great pain, although he had some pain. He seemed to be more in extreme discomfort, unable to find a restful position where his breathing would not be so difficult, and he would not have the fear of it shutting down all together. He seemed to be able to breath better when he was sitting up than lying down.

    We did not realize that he was fighting death all day long; so long as he stayed up he could breathe; when he laid down, he was afraid he would die and quickly wanted to get up. However, when he was sitting up, he looked so tired and his back, shoulders and neck hurt, and he was bent over at the back and neck all day long as he sat up. He never slept all day long. Occasionally, he would look up to see who was there. During his last day, we all were there at one time or another (all except Ron who was not scheduled to come until April 17). Florian Frank also visited for several hours. We said the rosary. We sang some religious songs. We played a stupid game—who put the wiener in the frying pan. We talked to one another and to dad. We tried to make dad feel more comfortable. We all rubbed his back and neck many times that day, rubbed Eucerin skin creme on his back and neck, lifted him up and down as he wanted to get up and down, moved him forward on the bed as he slid down, raised and lowered the bed, etc. In retrospect, it seems to me that dad was trying to stay up because he felt more comfortable and because he was afraid he would die if he laid down and let go.

At some point, he just decided he was ready to go and then went very quickly. It was after we all left. I don't know if he wanted it that way or it just happened that way. I wished, as we all did, that we had been there at the moment of his death. It would have been a great privilege. I had talked to Sandy earlier (around 7:30pm) about dad's behavior and she said that she had seen several other people act like dad was acting as they were dying. I asked her when she thought it would be?

She said, "I am not God, I don't know but it will be soon after he decides he is ready to die." She said that he was fighting death all day and that he might fight for days yet, but then he might go suddenly. She said it was all up to him. After he died, she said that his dying alone was his final gift to us—saving us the grief of seeing him die. I think she was just trying to be nice, but who knows. I only know that I wish I had been there. I almost was, by about 5-10 minutes.

In retrospect, I should have seen signs too. He had asked me to put on his other sock. He always had the bad foot covered. He was cold in his feet and hands and arms. But, I thought that was because the air conditioning was on and the room was cold, and he was just sitting in his diaper and his T-shirt. I thought he seemed too strong to be dying soon. During the time I was with him alone, he told me he had to take a pee. I called for Sandy because I wasn't sure what to do. She didn't come right away so I found the plastic pea thing and was taking off his diaper when she came. I asked her what to do and did it for him. She let me do it; in fact, it seemed that she wanted me to do it for him. Perhaps it was part of her helping me to be a part of his dying process. Perhaps it was just accident.

When it was all over, I felt so glad that I had been there for the last two days and that I had been with him nearly all day that day. I was glad for him that his misery was over. I felt gratitude to Doris and Vernon, Virgie and Jan and Coleen who had spent so much time with him during the last years. I felt that he must be with mom. We had told him several times during the day, that mom would be waiting from him when he was ready. He had said over and over, "Jesus help me" during the day. I always thought it was for the pain, but I now think he was asking for help in dying. He might have been afraid, or he might have just been asking for help in dying soon. There are so many things I just don't know and never will.

8. LETTERS

Kurt Kraemer to Leo and Lucy, circa 1972-1974

L>R:vKim, Leo, Kurt and Lucy Kraemer

Norine was going to college at UCI for an undergraduate degree.

Dear Grandma and Grandpa.
How are you? It looks as if everyone is so busy, I must do the letter writing. If my writing seems a little sloppy, it's because I'm

writing with a three-inch pencil. Well, I suppose I should be letting you know what is happening.

Dad is working hard with his papers and trying to finish them before the research deadline. He is gone Friday and Saturday with classes that come in for the whole day. He is working hard, and the symptoms are showing up--grouchy, crabby and falls to sleep right after supper.

Mom is busy with her tests. School isn't getting much easier because she had to drop a class in "statistics." She still stays in hibernation in the office and you really don't know she's even there.

Sister is busy with her softball games and girl scouts. She has more and more friends dropping over every day now. And when she's not busy she's bugging me. She still detests practicing her piano, and seems to be getting rowdier.

I, well, I went to the doctor to see if anything was wrong with my back because it was hurting me. He told me I should rest. That means I can't play sports and ride my bike for one month. Dad says "Good, that'll give him time to become a scholar and will cut down the rate of flat tires." Our class has been taking advantage of the teachers, and apparently, we might have taken too much, because we may have lost our privileges for the rest of the year. Well that's about all I know right now so I'll leave now.

    Your loving grandson, Kurt

Letters in Retirement

[Leo seldom wrote letters, and when he did, they were short. Below is a longer one:]

Leo to Ken and Norine, September 1973

Lucy and I are fully retired now. I am so busy now. I don't get reading done. Painted the living room and hall and one upstairs bed room. I work a few hours a week at the shop. Today I asked Ma how she got along all these years without me. We play cards about two times a week. We were invited to Florida by the Gilbert

Bauers to stay with them. If we want to spend money for traveling it would be California, to Ken and Norine's house. I hear your roof is leaking. If you get it fixed, get a local Builder to do the work. And stay there to watch the work being done. The contractor may be OK, but the workers always try to get by with something. If you do the whole roof there is a new insulation - Styrofoam. It comes in different thickness 1 ½" and 2" and 4' x 8' sheets.

I would like to come out to do the work but I'm afraid it would be too big a job for me. Lucy has been sick with a cold all week. Being retired is a big job. I have a hard time to get all my work and reading done. We are getting a new rug for the living room and the living room rug goes in the bedroom.

Stop in to see us some Sunday when you drive by.
Love Leo
Hi to Kim and Kurt.

Leo Kraemer to Phyllis Avenson, circa 1980

Dear Phyllis
Dad Here

Forget about golfing so early in spring. R.J., Kathy and kids were here this weekend. Jan and family stopped in after church. The house really was full. Saturday, we had pork chops & Sunday we had steak. They were here only 25 1/2 hours. It also snowed some 24 hours while they were here. Dan and Tim didn't come.

Saturday night the firemen had Spring Fever [name of a fund-raising event]. Thirty dollars a couple for dinner and all you wanted to drink.

I was to Madison last week, to find out about my physical condition. Everything <u>is back to normal</u>. How I hate that word.

The <u>little</u> Doll's toe is nice and straight. Hope it stays that way. Now she can wear shoes again. Last week we were to Toots and Herman's for cards. Tuesday and Thursday there were here for cards. Give us a short <u>buss</u> when you are coming.

Love, Dad

Lucy to Norine and Ken, 1987

April 1987

Dear Ken and Norine

The saxophone player made such a mess of his playing "Perfect Strangers" but someone said bad sax is better than no sax at all. Leo said his sax wasn't worth a dime. He takes his medication, then goes for a walk. He is supposed to take it one hour before he walks. I take mine immediately after meals, then I judge when its one hour.

Last night I went for a walk and when I got back, Leo was nowhere around, so I went upstairs because I always wash his back, and low and behold, he was sound asleep in the tub. He can sleep by the TV for hours then goes to bed and sleeps till about two o'clock, and then thinks it's terrible if he can't sleep all night. Well, I sat down on the John, because the heater was on the chair, and I just wanted to see how long he would sleep. He was blowing steam and his tummy went up and down. The tub was full to the top. I got tired of waiting so I stuck my fingers in the water and flicked it at him but with no response. I waited a little and tried it several more times; finally, he sat up and I said I would thank God if I could sleep like you can. I take a sleeping pill almost every night. Last night I was so scared I crawled in bed with him; I had such a horrible dream. Well I'm closing. I'm still tired from the horrible dream.

Love you all, Mom

Leo Kraemer to Phyllis Avenson, circa 1990

[Phyllis: Mom wanted dad to write us girls and he said he didn't know what to write so she told him to write what he did all day. The letter is probably 15 years old or so (2005).]

Sept. 24
Out of bed at 7:00 o'clock.
Drained hot water boiler.
Started taking boiler apart.

Found safety valve leaking.
Got new safety valve and put in same.
Fixed water valve on shut off pipe.
Refilled water boiler with water.
Ate breakfast.
Went to shop and office for two hours to visit.
Went golfing with Doris for one and half hours.
Had lunch.
Went to shop to grind drill bits for two hours.
Washed car.
Chammied same.
Peeled potatoes and fried same.
Fixed washing machine.
Went to bank to cash check.
And to Jan's house to play cards.
    Dad

[In contrast to Leo, Lucy was a faithful weekly writer of letters several pages long, but her letters got shorter and shorter over time. One memorable letter written in 1995 simply said:]

"At 91 years, we are both still here. We had only eleven operations each during those 91 years. I have only six ailments and dad has three."

9. MEMORIES ABOUT LEO

The following memories of Leo, or Leo and Lucy, by family members.

Memories, Memories (50th Anniversary, 1986, from Phyllis)
Let's go back a few years
We'll bring you some laughs and maybe some tears
So please share in our memories.

O April showers will bring May flowers. Time for May altars and songs of Mary.
We used a lot of cowslips, violets, candles, walked around the halls
And sang these songs we will now sing one for you.

Cookies, cookies
Mother made lots of them
We all loved them especially the Lena kind
She kept them in a crock in the cellar
Whenever we went down to get something
We usually ate one or two or three or four or maybe more.

Doris do you remember the time you asked me to see if I could sneak some out. You had to be resourceful to get past Mom. She didn't miss much. When I came outside and handed the cookies to you, you ate one and said, "How did you ever get these?" I said, "That's easy I just hid them in my bloomers."

Jolly old St. Nicolaus, came to us each year.
On December 6th it was
Wearing clothes of black
He stamped his stick out on the porch
And sometimes ran away, leaving sacks of popcorn balls, and peanuts for us too.

Ah yes, Christmas time. How exciting... Closing the door December 23 and tying it shut, covering all the cracks and keyholes, but never quite good enough. We always tried to peek down the register to see if he had been there. No one could eat much supper on the 24th. Anticipation of opening the door was so great – to see the tree trimmed and the lights on and presents all around. Then midnight Mass for those of us who went. What a thrill to see the Christ child carried to the manger with the men's choir singing Stille Nacht [Silent Night].

Hail Mary full of grace, the Lord is with thee. Blessed are you among women and blest is the fruit of your womb – Jesus. Can anyone guess what's coming next. You're right. Rosary time. Remember when we brought the wooden kitchen chairs to rest on while kneeling to say the rosary. Jan and Ronnie were tots going from one chair to the other sometimes with a wash rag in their mouth or climbing on the back of one of us – anything for a distraction. Who remembers the block Rosary at Lucille Walsh's and then sometimes another one right after at Grace Heiser's.

Du Du Lic Mer in Herzen, etc. Beer steins, click glasses and sway. Many songs were sung over the years as we washed and wiped dishes, at Mary and Alphonse Kraemers, at our house while the kids played piano and...

Fried egg sandwiches from dad's lunch pail. Vanilla and chocolate sandwich cookies. Twinkies. Dad reading the comics from the Sunday paper to us kids laying on the floor in the living room. Our Sunday nickel and how we looked forward to that. Sitting on the front porch Sunday afternoons after the ballgames. Cutting out dolly dingles. Tents made with old blankets in the back yard. Canning radishes in salt water. Hanging dish towels under the old wooden kitchen table to make partitions and playing house. Playing school and church in the basement. Playing confession in the storeroom under the steps. Ken as the priest with the Beretta and whole outfit. Swimming at the BAB. Calling the operator on the phone at the Stockyard to get the time. Dad making popcorn. Going fishing to "Sophie's hole." Swimming at Rainbow Gardens. Those wonderful dynamite boxes and all the things we used them for. Frying down pork in the basement. Rings of bologna hanging on the back porch. Thank you, Mom and Dad, for creating memories.

Washing cards - Phyllis Avenson, 2016
Dad and Mom always washed the cards because they were so dirty and sticky. They would dry them by hand and then put cornstarch on them, so they would be slippery. I started buying them lots of cards, but they still washed them.

Leo not sure if Lucy went to heaven (Phyllis Avenson, 2-16)
Kris and Wayne stopped last night after we got off at the hospital with pizza and we played cards, then were talking about different things. I brought up dying and going to heaven and giving my thoughts on that and then it reminded me of what dad said so I will tell you and you can use it or not. I was sitting in the assisted living with him after mom died and he said he is worried that

Mom didn't go to heaven. When I asked him why he said he didn't get a sign. After his sister died (I don't remember which one anymore.) he said he was in a room and there were no flowers anywhere or outside and he smelled roses. He felt that was a sign that she was giving him from heaven and he hasn't received anything from Mom. I don't know if he ever did as I didn't think to ask. I remember when Leonard died, and he loved rainbows as did his family. When we all came out of the funeral parlor after the first viewing, there was a big rainbow in the sky and they all felt it was a sign from Leonard.

EKS Update, 1996 - *Where are they now?*
"Leo Kraemer began his 46-year career with EKS in 1929. Through the years he did a variety of jobs for the company. For the first 14 years he was a Shovel Operator. Later he became a Foreman and held that position for 22 years. Prior to his retirement in 1975, Leo built crushers and fabricated and repaired machinery. Some of the jobs he was involved with included digging the church basement of St. Luke's Church in Plain. He also helped construct Highway 23 from Spring Green to Plain, along with work on Highway 14. Later in 1944 he was involved with crushing rock for the airport in Covington, Kentucky. A year later he was in Madison working on the airport, and then to Camp McCoy to build roads and runways.

One of the things Leo is most proud of during his years with EKS is the amount of yardage he could produce with the equipment he had to work with. He was able to crush 500 yards of gravel per day more than previous foremen. Leo has been active his whole life. After his retirement, and with a little coaching from his daughter, Doris, he took up golf. He played golf until he was 85, when his back wouldn't let him lift the clubs out of the car. His lowest score was 42 on the Plain Westbrook Hills Golf Course. His own unique swing, not found in any manuals, kept his score in the 40 and low 50 range. You couldn't beat his score for not swinging like a pro.

At 91 years old, Leo and his wife, Lucy, recently moved into their new home in Plain. Leo currently titles himself a Domestic

Engineer and Nurse who takes care of his wife, beside engineering the laundry, cooking and cleaning. He is known by the neighborhood kids as "a good fudge maker."

Virginia Fleming – Dad and horses

Dad liked horses, but also had problems with them.
Once he had the horses hitched up to the wagon ready to go to town when they decided to take off on their own. First, they reared up and then they headed straight for the barn. They ran into the barn and kept hitting their heads on the ceiling beams. By the time they made it to the other end of the barn they figured out they had to keep their heads down. From then on, they never went near the barn again.

Another time, dad and mom were loading hay into the barn using the horse tied to a rope that ran up to a pulley at the top of the barn. A big claw was at one end, which would grab a pile of hay, and the horse was at the other end. The horse would go out from the barn and pull the hay up to the second level where somebody would pull it into the hayloft. Mom and dad were talking to each other after they had come in with a load of hay, and the horse which was already tied to the pulley system was getting restless. Suddenly, he took off running and when he got to the end of the rope, it jerked him back and he fell over backwards. After that, he came back to mom and dad and waited patiently.

One horse was very stubborn and didn't want to work, so dad got mad and got the shotgun and let go at the horse's rear end. The shot scared the horse and put a few shots in its rear, and he had no problems with the horse from then on.

Had two grays named Dan and Roudy and two others. Two were young and were not broken in. Usually, you take one old one and one young one and put them together to break them in. Dad took the two young ones and put them on the wagon together. They took off running and he could barely get in the wagon, but he jumped on while it was moving and climbed in. They ran for about an hour and he could not stop them until they got tired out and then were OK from then on. He thought that the wagon was going to tip over several times on that wild ride.

When dad was young, he went out and hitched up the horses to go to church. He was barefoot. Old Charlie stepped back and stepped right on the sides and front of dad's foot. The horse had iron horseshoes. Then dad had to put his shoes on to go to church. Dad remembers his foot swelling and he didn't dare say anything because he wasn't supposed to go near the horses.

Around 1993, dad and mother moved from the old Martin house to a house in Westbrook because it was too dangerous for mother to go up and down stairs and getting more and more difficult for dad too.

"Welcome to my pad," circa 1993

Norine and I happened to be home for a week or weekend on the day dad brought mother to the new house for the first time. She had been in Greenway Manor in Spring Green recovering from a broken hip and knew nothing about it. When he brought her into the house, she did not understand why we were there and he said, "Welcome to our new pad" and kissed her. Mother just looked around not fully understanding what was going on. She was already suffering from dementia. After a tour of the house, we were sitting in the living room and mother finally put it all together and she said, *"Dad, you sure have bought yourself a peck of trouble this time."*

During this same time, Father Mike Resop visited the new house to see it for the first time. After she gave him a tour, mother asked if they could get the anointing of the sick. He said that he thought that Leo and Lucy "already had so many anointing's that they would slide right into heaven," but that he would do it again.

Leo and Lucy in Park Ave. house, circa 1980

Source: Doris Bindl.

Leo and Lucy's 70th Anniversary, Chris Avenson, 1996

Our annual summer trip to Wisc. to see Grandma and Grandpa was always much anticipated. ...We'd pull up to the curb and rush inside to the smell of raised donuts that Grandma had always made. Grandpa would get up from his chair where he usually sat reading the paper. And the hugs would go all around. Then upstairs we'd fly to check out "our" room and then mom and dad's. You know, the one with the closet where the safe was hidden. They always got the room that looked out on the street. I always wanted that room and finally on our honeymoon, Wayne and I got to sleep in it. I found out that it's the noisiest spot to try to sleep what with being the main drag for all the cars that would drive by with noisy teenagers shouting out the windows.

Then it was on to the big old bathroom to check out the old bathtub.

By now it was time to go downstairs for some bologna and cheese.

When it was time for us to go to bed, we'd always sneak out and try to spy on the grown-up's downstairs through the floor vents. We thought were so tricky. I was so disappointed when they carpeted over them.

And I remember mom crying when it was time to say goodbye. I never understood until I got a little older and wiser.

We love you Grandpa and Grandma.
Kris, Wayne and the kids

Leo and Lucy's 70th Anniversary, David Avenson, 1996

What I remember most about grandma and grandpa is the long ride down to Plain and every time when we got there we would have ring bologna and fried potatoes. It is still my favorite meal. Then when we would get up early in the morning to go back up North, grandma would have made raised donuts for us to eat in the morning. I also remember molasses cookies with raisons in the middle. D.A.

Visit to the old Peter Kraemer farm {Leo, Ken and Norine, 1999)

Norine and Ken visited the old Peter Kraemer farm with Leo in October 1999 and wrote the following:

Dad's big reaction to seeing the house and all the buildings was that they seemed so small. He remembered them as being much larger. He also remembered all the rooms and what had been where in the house. He noticed the changes that the current owners had made to the house. He was very excited, pleased and wide-eyed at the experience. He walked the entire house, barn and grounds on his own and with a spring in his step. We were afraid that he might fall.

Dad mentioned that, to make cash money, Pete shaved hoops for barrels and cut railroad ties with a double-sided ax. The barrel hoops were rough because they would still have the bark on the outside side of the hoops.

All the buildings on the farm are the original buildings. They did not tear any down and they did not build any new ones. They added a large open room on to one side of the house but otherwise have kept it pretty much as it was originally. The living room floor is original as is much of the kitchen and downstairs bedroom. A porch has been built on the barn side of the house.

The granary has been converted into a dormitory for the grandchildren. It is amazing, but one could still smell the grain in the building even after drywall had been put over the walls. The gain smell apparently has penetrated the wood deeply.

The machine shed is still just that. The smoke house is used to store wood. The corn crib has had a kiln built inside it for firing pottery. The grape arbor has been kept and expanded.

The barn is in original condition except that it has been converted to a workshop and split into two divisions with a new wall between them. The spring that come out of the side of the hill by the barn is still producing fresh water and goes in two directions from the hill—one towards the house and another towards the barn where there is water for the animals.

When we entered the granary, which had been converted to a dormitory, we could still smell the grain. The original cuts in the ceiling for the grain shoots were still there. The original steps to the second level were still there. The upstairs had been used for storing wheat and the downstairs had been divided into two areas for storing barley and rye.

Current (1999) owners of the Peter Kraemer Farm

The Peter Kraemer farm is now owned by the Batson family. Batson was an etiologist for a commercial company in Illinois and retired and came to the farm to be a potter and sculptor. All his sculpture is made from the land or the farm. He uses wood and branches on the farm to make playful sculptures like a cat over the kiln entry, a fish in the barn, a bell tower in the arbor, etc. He makes metal sculpture out of things like the milk stanchions or old farm equipment. They bought 80 acres of the farm, including the buildings and some woods in 1963 and were living there when we visited in October 1999.

Imitation of Elvis -Virginia 2014
We were playing cards at The Meadows and a program came on the TV featuring Elvis Presley. One lady said she didn't like him and I said I really liked his voice. Several comments made by others. Suddenly Dad stood up and very serious faced he did his imitation of Elvis and his gyrations. He was funny at age 96. Of course, everyone laughed.

Dad always had this thing about fat people. He always said Mom was getting fat while she was in the nursing home. Her muscle was breaking down. He always made comments about me too when I came back from California.

Sundrop, Tom Forbes, 2015
Whenever we came to the house, he would mix drinks and put Sundrop in the drink.

Leo's Lettuce dressing - Paul Avenson. 2016
When I was in the Coast Guard I would stop to visit Leo and Lucy when I was traveling home to Minnesota. Leo would have my room ready for me and then would cook me dinner. Lucy could not really cook at this time in her life. We would have a drink together before dinner and talk about the old days. I can't remember everything we talked about, but mainly it was about what it was like growing up as a boy in Plain and stories from the past. Leo was a good cook and he would always make a salad with dinner. He made what he called "lettuce dressing" which was the best dressing I ever had. I asked him for the recipe and he hand wrote the recipe which I still have and have attached to this e-mail, so everyone can use it.

One story Leo told me stands out. It was a hot summer day and his father was working in the fields and asked Leo to go get him some water to drink. So, Leo went and got a bucket of water and was bringing it back to his dad in the fields. He passed by a pony in the field and it looked thirsty to him, so he let the pony drink out of the bucket. When the pony was done drinking water, he brought the bucket of water to his dad in the fields. His dad drank the water from the bucket and then said to Leo thank you, but how come you didn't fill the bucket with more water? Leo then told his dad that he let the pony drink from the bucket first. I can't remember what Leo said his dad did or said, but Leo sure chuckled about the story. Paul

> lettuce Dressing
> 1 cup sugar
> 1 teaspoon salt
> ½ cup ~~sugar~~ vinegar
> ¼ cup veg. oil
> 1 ½ cup water
> ¼ teaspoon pepper
> shake

10. FAMILY IN THE CENSUS

The 1930 Census Leo and Lucy starting their family with daughter Virginia. It also shows that they were living in town, renting and paying $8.75 per month in rent, which is consistent with what Leo reported earlier ($8.00) in Chapter 4. The Census, shows that he was driving truck, also consistent with the way he described quarry work earlier.

1930 Census

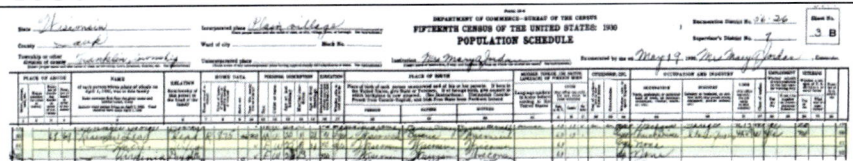

Kraemer, Leo, head, renting $8.75 per month, no radio, not on a farm, male, white, age 25, married at 21, not attending school, able to read and write, born WI, father and mother born Germany, speaks English, truck driver, State quarry, worker, employee, not a veteran
Lucy, wife, female, white, age 25, married at 21, not attending school, able to read and write, born WI, father born Germany, mother born Wisconsin, can speak English
Virginia, daughter, female, white 2½, single, not attending school

The 1940 Census shows that the family was nearly complete with all but the youngest child, Ron, who would be born in 1942. It also shows that Leo had completed 8th grade whereas Lucy only completed 6th grade. It is also interesting that the $1600 annual income is consistent with Leo's tax statement ($1626.55) for the year shown earlier in Chapter 4.

1940 U.S. Census, Village of Plain

Kraemer, Leo, head, own home, $3,000 value, male, white, 35, married, not attending school, highest grade completed 8, born WI, living same house 1935, yes, worked 40 hours, laborer, building, worked 40 hours in 1939, wage worker in private work, $1600 annual salary, no other income
Lucy, wife, female, 35, married, not attending school, highest grade completed 6, born WI, living same house 1935
Virginia, daughter, female, white, 12, single, attending school, highest grade completed 6
Doris, daughter, female, white, 9, single, attending school, highest grade completed 2
Phyllis, daughter, female, white, 6, single, not attending school
Kenneth, son, male, white, 3, single, not attending school
Jan, son, male, white, 1, single, not attending school

Although Leo and Lucy had housekeepers, the Censuses do not show them living in the same house. They were usually only temporary, worked between the Census years and/or lived at home. For example, Veronica Kraemer could walk a few blocks from her home.

11. ANCESTORS AND DESCENDANTS

Leo's ancestors came from the Oberpfalz region of Bavaria, Germany. Historically, all the Kraemers were weavers or weavers and subsistence farmers (1/2 farmers) from 1649 until Paul Kraemer immigrate to America in May 1866. As subsistence farmers, the Kraemers had just enough land to grow flax for their linen weaving, get lumber for firewood and building, raise a few animals and plant a garden. At most, they accumulated about 12 acres of land, but it was scattered around the countryside.

Please see the book *Wisconsin Kraemers book series. Part I, The old world of Bavaria* for a rich history of the Kraemers in Bavaria. *Wisconsin Kraemers II* presents the history of the Kraemers in the new world of America, specifically Paul and Walburga Kraemer and their children. *Wisconsin Kraemers III* delves into the history of Peter Kraemer, his three wives and their children. Leo was the youngest child that lived. These books can be found at www.CreateSpace.com, www.amazon.com or Plain and Spring Green public libraries.

Peter's parents: Paul Kraemer and Walburga Stangl

Paul and Walburga were both the children of weavers. They lived in villages about 4-5 miles apart, Irlach for Paul and Heinrichskirchen for Walburga. The latter had its own church whereas Irlach only had a small chapel and belonged to the parish in the town of Tiefenbach.

Irlach & villages around within 5KM circle

They married in 1854, the same year that Paul's father and brother died within a week of one another from pneumonia. These deaths meant that Paul inherited the family farm, but he also inherited his father's second family – a stepmother and five children.

Irlach with other villages in background

Photo by Heinrich Reinermann.

As a result, Paul and Walburga gave ten years to caring for the step-mother and children until they all had left home and the step-mother died. Within the year of her death, they left for America and Wisconsin.

A year after they arrived in June 1867, they found a 120-acre farm east of Plain – 10 times the size of their farm in Irlach. The farm had been tended and built-up by another family for ten years before that husband and father died in the Civil War and the widow had to sell the farm. Paul acquired more land over time and built-up the farm threefold. They had seven children who all became farmers in the Franklin and Spring Green Townships and had large families of their own. The location of the farm in Wisconsin is show on the 1893 plat map in Chapter 1

Grace's parents: Adam Ring and Frances Roetzer

The Rings came from the same region and lived in another village only two miles from Irlach. They were even smaller farmers than the Kraemers in Germany. Adam Ring was a weaver and a 1/8 farmer (about 6 acres of land) who lived at house #24 in Haag. Both families were part of the Tiefenbach Parish, so it is possible that the Rings and Kraemers knew one another in Bavaria.

The aerial photo below shows the location of house #24 within Haag. In the 1800s, the farm-in-town consisted of a house, stable, barn, garden and possibly an animal yard, and was completely fenced with a stone wall. There also were a few fields outside of town for growing flax for weaving.

The village had a small chapel in the 1800s, but major events (masses, baptism, marriage, funeral) occurred in Tiefenbach where the Catholic church was located. A church was built in Haag after World War II (see arrow).

The Rings immigrated to America in 1883 with eight children and settled on an 80-acre farm in Troy Township very near to the Paul Kraemer family. They attended the same one-room school house in their neighborhood and belonged to the St. Luke Catholic parish in Plain.

Aerial photo of Haag

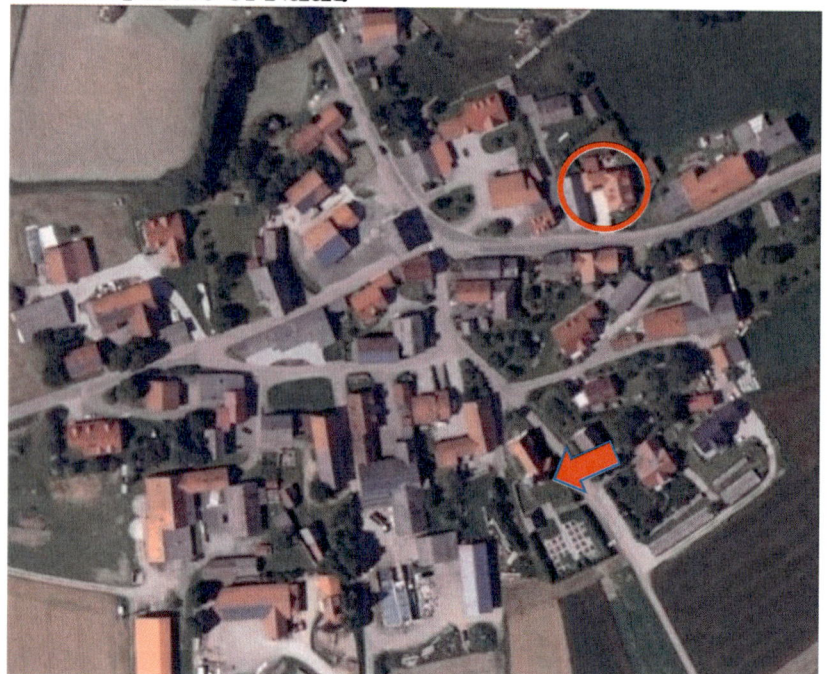

Source: Google maps, last accessed May 2017. Arrow pointing to church and cemetery.

Haag village and church

Photo by Ken Kraemer, 2014. Arrow is pointing to church built after WWII.

Leo Kraemer and Lucy Bauer family tree

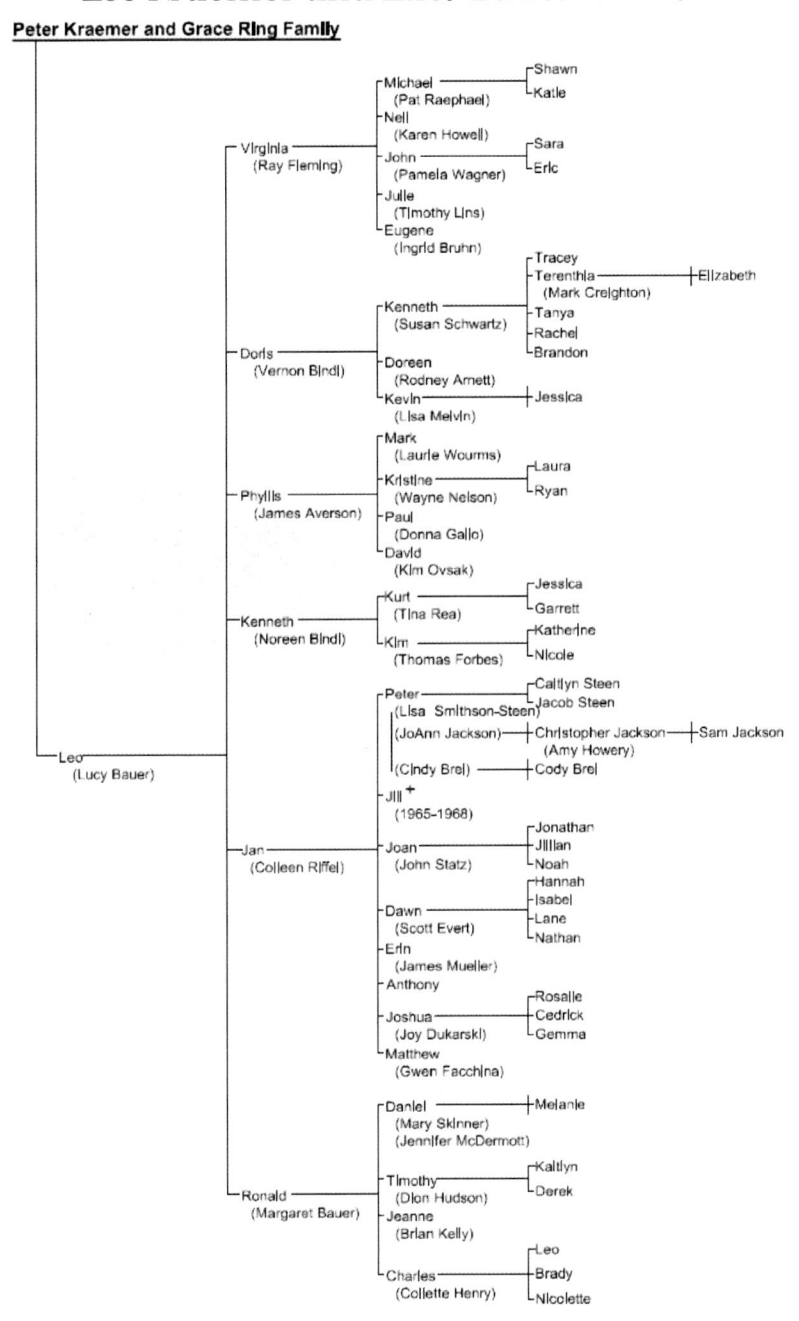

Peter Kraemer and Grace Ring Family

- Leo (Lucy Bauer)
  - Virginia (Ray Fleming)
    - Michael (Pat Raephael)
      - Shawn
      - Katie
    - Neil (Karen Howell)
    - John (Pamela Wagner)
      - Sara
      - Eric
    - Julie (Timothy Lins)
    - Eugene (Ingrid Bruhn)
  - Doris (Vernon Bindl)
    - Kenneth (Susan Schwartz)
      - Tracey
      - Terenthia (Mark Creighton) + Elizabeth
      - Tanya
      - Rachel
      - Brandon
    - Doreen (Rodney Arnett)
    - Kevin (Lisa Melvin)
      - Jessica
  - Phyllis (James Averson)
    - Mark (Laurie Wourms)
    - Kristine (Wayne Nelson)
      - Laura
      - Ryan
    - Paul (Donna Gallo)
    - David (Kim Ovsak)
  - Kenneth (Noreen Bindl)
    - Kurt (Tina Rea)
      - Jessica
      - Garrett
    - Kim (Thomas Forbes)
      - Katherine
      - Nicole
  - Jan (Colleen Riffel)
    - Peter (Lisa Smithson-Steen) (JoAnn Jackson) (Cindy Brei)
      - Caitlyn Steen
      - Jacob Steen
      - Christopher Jackson — Sam Jackson (Amy Howery)
      - Cody Brei
    - Jill † (1965-1968)
    - Joan (John Statz)
      - Jonathan
      - Jillian
      - Noah
    - Dawn (Scott Evert)
      - Hannah
      - Isabel
      - Lane
      - Nathan
    - Erin (James Mueller)
    - Anthony
    - Joshua (Joy Dukarski)
      - Rosalie
      - Cedrick
      - Gemma
    - Matthew (Gwen Facchina)
  - Ronald (Margaret Bauer)
    - Daniel (Mary Skinner) (Jennifer McDermott)
      - Melanie
    - Timothy (Dion Hudson)
      - Kaitlyn
      - Derek
    - Jeanne (Brian Kelly)
    - Charles (Collette Henry)
      - Leo
      - Brady
      - Nicolette

Family tree chart from Marty Kraemer, 2017.

References:

Leo Kraemer interviews, 1986-87, 1988.

Leo Kraemer, phone discussions, 1999, Jan 5, 2001

Virginia Fleming, Notes from discussion, 2001.

Virginia Fleming, Experience at The Meadows, undated.

Blau, Debbie and Kenneth L. Kraemer, 2014, *Kraemer in Amerika*, CreateSpace, an Amazon Company.

Geesaman, Claire, 1995, *A Kraemer Chronicle*. Madison, WI: Edgewood University Press.

Kraemer, Kenneth L., 2015, *Wisconsin Kraemers I: The old world of Bavaria, CreateSpace, an Amazon Company.*

Kraemer, Kenneth L., 2017, *Wisconsin Kraemers II: The new world of America, CreateSpace, an Amazon Company.*

Kraemer, Kenneth L., 2018, *Wisconsin Kraemers III: The twentieth century, CreateSpace, an Amazon Company.*

Kraemer, Kenneth L., 2015, *LUCY*, CreateSpace, an Amazon Company.

Kraemer, Edward and Sons, Where they are now? *EKS Update*, 1996 [A newsletter from Edward Kraemer and Sons]

Thering, Hildegarde, 1982, *A history of Plain, Wisconsin.*

Index

Places

Haag, 111-112
Irlach, 14, 109-114
Tiefenbach, 110-111

Franklin Township, 1893 map of, 12; location of Leo Kraemer rented farms, 36
Plain, Mike Ring store, 2; Joseph Kraemer, 7; buy house in, 18; Leo walk to school, 20; Reasers for picnics, 21; Plain band, 21; moonshine country, 26; Leo & Lucy house locations, 59; Palace Hall anniversary celebrations, 87-move to Westbrook, 59; 1930, 1940 census, 107-108.
Catholic school & public school, 19
Spring Green Township, map of, 12
Spring Green, Greenway, Manor & Lucy, 82, 86, 101; The Meadows and Leo, 86-88
Troy Township, 1892 map of, 12; location of Ring farm, 111

People

Avenson,
James, marriage to Phyllis Kraemer, 78-79

Bauer
Lucy, first real date & kiss, 25; marriage, 29-33; children, Greenway Manor,
Margaret, Lucy's mother, 30

Kathy, marriage to Ron Kraemer, 71-72
John W., carpenter, builder of Leo Kraemer house, 53f

Bindl
Vernon, and Doris, 75-77
Norine, and Ken, 79-82

Eckstein
Kate, third wife of Peter, marriage to Pete, 7-9; death of children, 17; caring for John Kraemer's kids, 25; perception by children, 16-17

Fleming, Ray, work with, 48; marriage to Virginia Kraemer, 74; visiting in retirement, 90

Frank
Joseph, dancing in new barn, 30
Ted, married to sister Esther, work for Ted before marriage, 35
Clemens, husband of Anna, care for Pete, 16, farming, butcher shop, 35; work for EKS, 42-43

Kraemer
Anna, sister of Leo, 17; wife of Clemens Frank, care for Pete, 16; family photo, 18
Anton, brother of Leo, 17
Albert, brother of Leo 17; family photo, 18; work outside the farm, 27
Alphons, brother of Leo, 17, family photo, 18; work for EKS, 51, 57; singing at his house 107

Benjamin, brother of Leo, 17; family photo, 18; purchase of family farm, 17-18
Doris, marriage to Vernon Bindl, 75-77
Edward, brother of Leo 17; family photo, 18; loan to Leo for house, EKS (Edward Kraemer & Sons),
Elizabeth, sister of Leo, 17; family photo, 18
Esther, sister of Leo, 17; family photo, 18
Frank, brother of Leo, 17; family photo, 18; purchase of farm, 17
Jan, and Colleen Riffle, 81, 83
Kenneth, and Norine Bindl, 79-82
Leo, quiet, independent, vi; loved Lucy, vi; attachment to aunt Frances, vi; dream of owning a farm, vii; birth, mother Grace, 1; Ring family, 2; father Pete, 2-3; Paul Kraemer family photo, 3; Grace & Pete wed photo, 5; siblings, 6; Pete Kraemer family, family photo, 8-9; Leo timeline 10; Leo photo collage, 11; location family farms, 12; Grace photos, 22; aunt Frances 23-25; meeting step-mother, 25; memories, 26; church, school, picnics, 26-29; first car, 25-26; marriage, 38-42; EKS work years, 47; shovel operator, 48; foreman 51; bunk house life, 55; shop work, 56; wages, 58; feelings about work, 59; injuries, 59; children, 61-71; weddings, 73-83; retirement, 84; anniversaries 85-89; Westbrook, Greenway Manor, The Meadows, 91-94; death and postscript, 96; ancestors & descendants, 119-123.

Veronica, housekeeper, 56, 61, 109
Phyllis, birth, 63; 69; 74-76; wedding, 78-79; 87, 90, 98-99, 104
Ronald, 68; 71-72; marriage to Kathy Bauer, 84

Riffle, Colleen, marriage to Jan Kraemer, 81-83

Ring
Adam, family photo, 2; home in Haag, Bavaria, 120-121
Anna, first wife of Peter, family photo, 12; wedding photo, 13
Grace, second wife of Peter
Frances, sister of Anna & Grace, 1; married George P. Schutz, 2
Frances, child of Adam and Frances born & died in Germany

Roetzer, Frances mother of Anna, Grace & Frances, 1, 11, 120-121

Schutz
George P. (Sr.), 11
George (Jr.), 31, 33, 39, 40, 42, 43, 86

Weidner
Edward, husband of Frances Kraemer, death, 23
Frances Kraemer, wife of Edward, aunt of Leo,
Mary, daughter of Edward & Frances, 23
John (Jack), son of Edward & Frances, 22, 25

ABOUT THE AUTHOR

Leo Adam Kraemer was born in 1905 on a small farm in the Wilson Creek area of Spring Green Township, a few miles south of Plain. He lived to be 97 years old, dying of old age in 2002 at The Meadows in Spring Green. He was the youngest in a family of ten children whose mothers were sisters. He never knew his mother as she died when he was two years old. Although he wanted to be a farmer, the depression and life interfered, and he ended up working on road construction for 44 years. Leo was well liked by his fellow workers and a distinguished figure in his retirement and old age, well-known and -liked in the community of Plain.

ABOUT THE EDITOR

Kenneth L. Kraemer is one of Leo's sons and Professor Emeritus at the University of California, Irvine. He was away from Plain most of his adult life, but had the privilege during 1986-87 and later of reminiscing in person with Leo about his life, which enabled this story to be written. He can be reached at and welcomes comment. He lives at 8 Needlegrass, Newport Coast, CA 92657.

AUTHOR AND EDITOR, CIRCA 1938

Made in the USA
Lexington, KY
18 September 2019